Maliha Abidi

RISE

Extraordinary
Women of Colour
Who Changed
the World

SAQI

Just like moons and like suns,
With the certainty of tides,
Just like hopes springing high,
Still I'll rise.

From 'Still I Rise'
by Maya Angelou

To Papa and Aski

Contents

Preface

Rise introduces 100 extraordinary women of colour from around the globe, whose lives have spanned millennia, and more than thirty countries. These women are an inspiration to me, as I hope that they will be to you, too.

Growing up, I rarely came across positive stories of women who looked like me or who I could identify with, culturally or otherwise. I wanted to create *Rise* so that other women of colour could find themselves, and empowerment, in a book. I wanted to honour these incredible female scientists, activists, leaders and artists who have worked both behind the scenes and under public scrutiny to make the world a better place.

Women from all walks of life are included here. Despite challenges, they rose to dizzying heights in a wide range of fields. From Esther Afua Ocloo, the entrepreneur with a homemade marmalade business who went on to found Women's World Banking, and Yusra Mardini, the athlete who fled civil war on a sinking boat, then swam in the Olymp ics; to Mae C. Jemison, an astronaut chosen from thousands of other candidates; these women prove that we can reach for the stars.

While some of the women included in *Rise* – Rosa Parks, Michelle Obama, Frida Kahlo, for example – are household names around the world; many others are still not well known, sometimes not even in their own countries. Though these iconic women's contributions are vitally important, it can sometimes feel like the same few are celebrated over and over again. There seems to be little space for more women of colour in mainstream media, resulting in a mis- or under-representation of Black, Arab, Indigenous, Asian, Brown or Mixed women. This feeds into the erroneous narrative that there are only a handful of role models who are women of colour. I hope that *Rise* shows how these remarkable women are, and always have been, on the frontline of change and creativity.

Being a woman of colour will mean something different to each one of us. What we do have in common, however, is an experience of discrimination both because of our gender and on account of our race. This is why intersectional feminism, a term coined by Kimberlé Crenshaw, was so close to my heart while creating *Rise* and why, although this book is predominantly a celebration, I chose not to diminish the hardships or traumas the women endured on their way to becoming incredible pioneers. To write only of their achievements would be doing a disservice to these women, and to my readers.

As I brought together these women's stories and portraits, I realised that there were many similarities between them. One pattern I noticed again and again was that they never gave up. This is true regardless of whether the woman was an athlete going for gold, a lawyer arguing for her client or one of the countless women fighting for recognition of their communities. And these trailblazing women not only stood up for themselves; they paved the way for so many others, too.

RISE

Aisholpan Nurguiv

Eagle Hunter
Born May 2001
Mongolia

For over a thousand years, the nomads of the Altai Mountains in Central Asia have hunted with eagles for food and fur during the harsh winters. The role of the hunter among Mongolian tribes has generally been a male preserve, and this tradition is typically passed on from father to son. But Aisholpan Nurguiv, a Mongolian Kazakh girl, had been fascinated by eagles since early childhood. She aspired to study medicine, but not before becoming an eagle hunter like her father.

Men in the community objected on the basis of their conviction that women are constitutionally unsuited to eagle hunting. Although Nurguiv was not the first female eagle hunter, women in this role are rare. Nurguiv's family, however, encouraged her. She and her father set out to acquire an eagle of her own. After scouting the mountains and finding a nest, Nurguiv descended the steep mountain face and captured an eaglet – a very difficult task.

'You were as brave as any man,' her father told her.

Nurguiv began training to compete in the annual Golden Eagle Festival in Ölgii, Mongolia – something no woman had ever done. Her father taught her how to summon her eagle, how to strengthen her bond with it and how to hunt with it.

On the day of the festival, more than seventy eagle hunters from several regions came to compete. Each was scored over several rounds. The first phase of the competition focused on equipment and horsemanship; the second, on summoning the eagle. In both rounds, Nurguiv scored highly. The third round judged the speed with which an eagle responds to the hunter's command. Nurguiv set a record time of five seconds.

Thirteen-year-old Nurguiv placed first, winning against older men with more experience. Her story was captured in an acclaimed 2016 documentary and she became renowned in Mongolia and beyond. She has continued to hunt with her father and still aims to become a doctor.

Alexandria Ocasio-Cortez

Congresswoman
Born 13 October 1989
United States of America

Alexandria Ocasio-Cortez was born and raised in New York City's Bronx borough. When she was five, her family moved to the suburb of Westchester, using all their funds plus borrowed money: her parents hoped to provide young Alexandria and her brother with better schooling and quality of life.

When Ocasio-Cortez was sixteen, her father was diagnosed with lung cancer. Times became difficult for the family, emotionally and financially, and they nearly lost their home. Ocasio-Cortez's mother cleaned houses, sometimes in exchange for university-preparation classes for her daughter.

Ocasio-Cortez gained admission to Boston University. Just before her sophomore year, during the financial crisis of 2008, her father died, and the family's situation worsened. They moved back to the Bronx, where Ocasio-Cortez joined them after graduating. She began working for an educational non-profit organisation, helping undocumented Latinx youths. She also worked as a bartender, taking extra shifts in order to support her family, recognising that their struggles were mirrored in the stories of many other local people.

In 2016, a political action committee called Brand New Congress approached Ocasio-Cortez to run for a seat in the US House of Representatives in 2018. (Her brother had nominated her; she was selected from 10,000 possible candidates.)

'Women like me aren't supposed to run for office,' she said in her campaign video. Ocasio-Cortez was widely underestimated: her opponent in the primary election had run unopposed for fourteen years. Her campaign was entirely grassroots-funded. She spoke about the adversity her community faced, including financial hardship, lack of healthcare and housing issues. Having confronted such problems while growing up, she was persuasive; voters realised that she would fight for them in government.

Ocasio-Cortez became the youngest congresswoman in US history and has earned a reputation for vigorously holding politicians and business interests to account.

Ama Ata Aidoo

Writer
Born 23 March 1940
Ghana

Ama Ata Aidoo has worked hard to further the progress of African women writers and is an internationally renowned writer herself. She grew up in a Ghanaian village steeped in local traditions. Her father, a Fante chief, established a school where Aidoo studied before attending high school in Cape Coast.

Vivid storytellers and artisans abounded in Aidoo's village. One storyteller who made a lasting impression on young Ama was her mother, whose Ghanaian folktales inspired much of Aidoo's work. Aidoo wanted to be a writer from an early age. When she was asked by a schoolteacher what she aspired to be when she was older, she replied, 'poet', without knowing quite why. The teacher was dubious, but gifted Aidoo an old typewriter to encourage her. Aidoo later earned a degree in English from the University of Ghana and wrote her first play, *The Dilemma of a Ghost*, in 1964.

Aidoo knew Ghana before and after it won independence from Britain in 1957 and witnessed the impact of social change, especially on women. Frequent themes in her writing include colonialism, the slave trade, polygamy, marital rape and the damage done to women through lack of rights.

A proud feminist, she has always taught works by African female writers as a professor in Ghana, and at Brown University in the US. In 2000 she founded Mbaasem ('Women's Words/Issues'), an organisation providing support to the next generation of African women writers. In 1982 she was appointed Ghana's Minister of Education, but resigned eighteen months later, realising that the male-dominated administration was not prepared to hear her ideas, which included access to education for all.

Aidoo's work consists of essays, plays, poetry, stories, novels and children's books. Her novels include *Our Sister Killjoy* (1977) and *Changes: A Love Story*, which won the 1992 Commonwealth Writers' Prize. A prize-winner across literary forms, her accolades also include the 1987 Nelson Mandela Award for Poetry.

Amal Clooney

Human Rights Lawyer
Born 3 February 1978
United Kingdom

Amal Clooney was only two years old when her family was forced to flee civil war in Lebanon. They made their new home in Britain. A gifted student, Amal obtained a scholarship to study Law at Oxford University, then moved to New York to earn an MA from New York University.

While working as a defence attorney for a prominent New York firm, she took on *pro bono* cases and became increasingly invested in their outcomes. Soon she quit her well-paying corporate job and applied for a clerkship at the International Court of Justice at The Hague. She also took on work in Beirut – her birthplace – before returning to the UK, where she joined the renowned Doughty Street Chambers in London to specialise in public international law, international criminal law and human rights.

Clooney's clients have included Mohamed Nasheed, the first democratically elected president of the Maldives, wrongfully charged with terrorism by the opposition; Khadija Ismayilova, a courageous investigative journalist from Azerbaijan imprisoned by her government; and Nadia Murad, survivor of the ISIS genocide of the Yazidis in Iraq. Clooney has also represented other Yazidi women and addressed the UN on this matter, urging it to prosecute ISIS militants. If the world took no action, she argued, the genocide would be forgotten by history; no proof would exist and the perpetrators would simply shave their beards and go on with their lives, while the victims will bear their trauma forever.

In 2017, UN Resolution 2379 was passed unanimously. Investigators were sent to Iraq to gather evidence against ISIS, exhuming mass graves to identify murdered Yazidis. Clooney's advocacy played a huge role in the passing of this resolution. It was the first step towards justice for many Yazidi families.

Amal Clooney has continued to speak up against human rights violations in different parts of the world, fiercely representing the victims of these crimes.

Amanda Gorman

Activist and Poet
Born 7 March 1998
United States of America

Poet and activist Amanda Gorman is a symbol of hope across the United States and beyond. Known for her work on issues of oppression, feminism and race, she delivered her poem 'The Hill We Climb' at the inauguration of US President Joe Biden in 2021. She hasn't looked back since.

In fact, Gorman climbed many hills before stepping up to the podium at Biden's inauguration. From childhood, Gorman had a speech impediment and an auditory processing disorder. Far from shying away from such obstacles, Gorman realised her impediment was also her strength and wrote into poems the words she struggled to share aloud. At just sixteen years of age, Gorman became the youngest inaugural poet in US history. Then, following a college scholarship, she went on to study Sociology at Harvard University.

In addition to studying, Gorman became a youth delegate for the United Nations and in 2016, founded the non-profit One Pen One Page, a youth writing and leadership programme. She uses her position to speak openly about the difficult realities that Black women and girls face.

The month after delivering 'The Hill We Climb', Gorman was racially profiled by a security guard. In response to the incident, she tweeted 'In a sense, he [the security guard] was right. I AM A THREAT: a threat to injustice, to inequality, to ignorance ... A threat and proud.'

On several occasions, Gorman has said that she intends to run for US president, and that, through political office, she hopes to turn her words into realities and actions. It is clear that Gorman's journey is only just starting. In an interview with Michelle Obama for *TIME* magazine, she spoke about how girls of colour are treated as 'lightning or gold in the pan', not as legacies. But Gorman is here to stay. 'I'm learning that I am not lightning that strikes once. I am the hurricane that comes every single year, and you can expect to see me again soon.'

Amna Al Qubaisi

Racing Car Driver
Born 28 March 2000
United Arab Emirates

Amna Al Qubaisi became a rising motorsports star in 2011, amid tensions surrounding women's rights in the region. Her chosen profession, and her clear talent for it, both inspired and intimidated many in the Middle East.

Racing was a huge part of Al Qubaisi's world from the beginning. She was born in Abu Dhabi, where her father, Khaled – a professional race car driver himself – noticed that Amna had a talent for racing. Amna and her sister grew up learning, talking and listening about racing, and attending races to cheer for their dad. At fourteen, Amna began her own career in motorsports with karting, supported by Khaled. Many of her contemporaries in the sport had begun more structured training than Amna had from an earlier age – some since they were five – and so she had to work hard to catch up. Fortunately catching up, and overtaking, is something Al Qubaisi is famously good at.

The other drivers competing against Al Qubaisi, who were predominantly male, underestimated her. They behaved in an unprofessionally aggressive manner towards her in races, attempting to push her out of the grid when she began an overtake. A competitive nature comes with being a racer, and no race car driver likes being overtaken; but the fact that a *girl* was speeding by these men struck a particular nerve. Al Qubaisi pushed back and proved herself to be a big name on the circuit.

Al Qubaisi competed nationally and internationally, making history on many occasions. At only seventeen, she became the first Arab woman to win the Rotax Max Challenge Championship for karting. At eighteen, she was the first Arab woman to test a Formula E car. At nineteen she became the first Arab woman to win the UAE Formula 4 race in the single-seater category.

Amna represents women in a male-dominated sport, and hopes she can inspire Arab women, in particular, to follow their motorsport racing instincts – and go for it.

Angela Davis

Scholar, Author and Activist
Born 26 January 1944
United States of America

Angela Davis was born in Birmingham, Alabama, in a neighbourhood called 'Dynamite Hill' because of notorious attacks by Ku Klux Klan racists. While studying in France as a teenager in 1963, she heard of the Birmingham church bombing in her home city that killed four girls, three of whom she knew.

Davis wanted to fight the daily injustices African Americans in the US faced. She became involved in the Civil Rights Movement, joining the Black Panther Party and the Communist Party – for which she was fired from her teaching position at University of California, Los Angeles. She challenged the wrongful termination in court and regained her post, along with numerous death threats. Concerned for her safety, she bought guns, and security escorted her everywhere.

Davis supported a campaign to release three African American prison inmates who had been charged with killing a guard in retaliation for the murder of three Black prisoners. Jonathan Jackson, part of Davis's security detail, was the brother of one of the accused men. During a courtroom hearing, he and three other men – using Davis's guns – held the judge and some jurors hostage, demanding the inmates' release. Police shot Jonathan, two other abductors and the judge. Investigators traced the guns back to Davis but, recognising a stitch-up, she went into hiding. She was apprehended by the police and realised that she was facing the death penalty.

While Davis awaited trial as the US's most famous political prisoner, thousands of people rallied to her side. While Aretha Franklin offered to pay her bail and John Lennon and Yoko Ono wrote a song about her; President Richard Nixon commended law enforcement for capturing this 'dangerous terrorist'. Then, in 1972, she won her case and her freedom.

Davis resumed her academic career as a distinguished professor and lecturer at several universities and continued her political activism. A feminist and progressive political icon, she has authored numerous books on racism, classism, sexism and prison abolition.

Aretha Franklin

Singer and Pianist
25 March 1942 – 16 August 2018
United States of America

'The Queen of Soul' was much more than a show-business nickname for Aretha Franklin. Her powerful charisma, passion and the intention with which she performed all lent her a mythical persona. She is inarguably one of the greatest American singers of all time.

Franklin was raised in Detroit. Her father, Reverend CL Franklin, was the pastor of New Bethel Baptist Church. New Bethel Baptist Church was at the heart of the Civil Rights Movement in that city and had a large African American congregation. Rev. Franklin's sermons inspired a community that often struggled to summon confidence.

The Franklin family contained many talented singers and musicians, but Aretha's genius stood out. At seven, she could play major chords on the piano and duplicate every note in a song after listening to it just once.

In 1952, her mother, a gospel singer, died, and Franklin, ten, found strength in singing. She gave her first solo performance at New Bethel, standing on a chair and marking the hearts of the thousands in attendance.

Success was inevitable. At twelve, Franklin toured with her father's gospel group; at fourteen, she recorded her first album. She soared naturally between jazz, gospel, R&B, rock and pop, releasing records across multiple genres. Her biggest hits came in the mid-1960s, with songs that stayed at the top of the charts. She toured widely, thrilling fans in the US, Europe and Latin America. One of her most famous hits, 'Respect' – a rendition of Otis Redding's original – became an anthem for the civil rights and women's rights movements alike. Franklin turned the patriarchal language of the song into a feminist declaration, though it struck a universal chord.

The first woman inducted into the Rock & Roll Hall of Fame; Franklin's career spanned decades. She sold millions of records and won eighteen Grammy awards.

Asima Chatterjee

Chemist
23 September 1917 – 24 November 2006
India

In British-ruled India, it was rare for women to pursue education beyond high school. However, Asima Mukherjee was a gifted student who loved chemistry and her father, a doctor with an interest in botany, was supportive of his daughter's continued studies. He taught Asima about the medicinal properties of indigenous plants and she was fascinated; as an adult scientist, she would continue to work closely with plants, making ground-breaking discoveries.

After graduating with honours in Chemistry, Mukherjee decided to continue her studies. Her family were not all supportive, and some of her more traditional relatives objected to the notion of her attending university alongisde men. But Mukherjee's parents continued to support her aspirations and she vindicated them, graduating at the top of her class and earning gold and silver medals. In 1944, she became the first woman to obtain a DSc from an Indian university.

The following year, Mukherjee married Baradananda Chatterjee, a physical chemist who shared his bride's passion for chemistry. Their daughter Julie would go on to study sciences as well.

Asima Chaterjee developed anti-epileptic and anti-malarial drugs, and identified vinca alkaloids as cancer-cell inhibitors, thereby improving the efficacy of chemotherapy. Her accomplishments are all the more impressive, given that laboratories in India then were not well funded and often lacked adequate research equipment.

Chatterjee paved the way for many other women in science. She founded the Department of Chemistry at Lady Brabourne College in Kolkata and became Honorary Professor of Chemistry at the University of Calcutta. In the US, she worked alongside world-renowned scientists at the University of Wisconsin and Cal Tech and later also lectured throughout Europe. She received many accolades, including the 1975 Padma Bhushan Award – one of the highest civilian honours in India.

Her career spanned six decades, during which she nurtured students, wrote over 400 papers and saved countless lives through her discoveries.

Autumn Peltier

Water Activist
Born 27 September 2004
Canada

Autumn Peltier is a water activist. Along with her community, the Anishinaabe people of Wiikwemkoong Unceded Territory on Manitoulin Island (on the shores of Lake Huron), Peltier believes that water is alive, with a spirit.

Peltier and her sisters were raised with deep Anishinaabek values by their single mother. Another strong woman in Peltier's life was her great-aunt Josephine Mandamin, Chief Water Commissioner of the Anishinaabe Nation, who dedicated her life to water protection and founded the Mother Earth Water Walk initiative.

Peltier was engaged with the issue of water protection from an early age, aware that in her own region, and in millions of communities around the world, clean water – a basic human right – is threatened by the oil industry and factories releasing toxic waste into the water supply. Peltier began speaking about this issue in her community, persisting despite bullying and indifference.

After seeing Peltier speak at a protest that shut down two motorways in 2016, an Anishinaabe regional chief invited her to present a ceremonial sacred bundle to Canadian Prime Minister Justin Trudeau at a First Nations assembly in Ottawa. Overcome with emotion and unable to give a prepared speech because of time constraints, Peltier told Trudeau (who had just approved a new pipeline), 'I'm very unhappy with the choices you've made.'

Despite her young age, Peltier has achieved much and worked relentlessly to bring awareness to her people and the issues of fresh, clean water availability. In 2017, Peltier was nominated for the International Children's Peace Prize. In 2018, she addressed the UN General Assembly on World Water Day, observing that, although Canada is a developed country, her people live in developing-country conditions. She continues to spread awareness throughout Canada on behalf of fifty-seven outstanding advisories in thirty-seven First Nations, and spoke again at the UN in 2019.

Carrying on her great-aunt's legacy, Peltier became the Anishinaabe Nation's Chief Water Commissioner at the age of fourteen. As Peltier has said, 'We cannot eat money or drink oil.'

Ava DuVernay

Filmmaker
24 August 1972
United States of America

The American filmmaker Ava DuVernay learned early on that if she wanted to make films, she'd have to rely only on herself. A journalist by training, DuVernay became a junior film publicist before opening her own public-relations firm. Following a 'wow, I could do that' moment on the set of a Hollywood production in 2004, her career as a director began. She was the first Black woman to win the US Dramatic Directing Award at the Sundance Festival, and to be nominated for both the Golden Globe and Academy Awards for directing.

DuVernay grew up in Compton, south of Los Angeles, and attended the University of California earning her degree in English and African American Studies. She was thirty-two when she decided to become a filmmaker, and taught herself, buying books, watching DVDs with directors' commentaries, and writing screenplays during the evenings and weekends. While continuing to run her PR company, she used her savings to make short films, documentaries and feature films. *I Will Follow* (2011) created a stir, and *Middle of Nowhere* (2012) won her the Sundance award. In *Selma* (2014), she depicted the circumstances and personalities around the 1965 civil rights march in Alabama, making her a contender for the Golden Globe.

13th, for which DuVernay earned an Academy Award berth, is a hard-hitting documentary that takes viewers on a journey from the early days of slavery to the era of mass incarceration that many Black Americans face today. The documentary also reveals police brutality and racism in the US judicial system.

DuVernay closed her agency in 2011, devoting herself full time to making films. Not one for second-guessing herself, she also sold her house.

'I just realised that I need to work without permission,' she has said. 'As long as you're asking people to help you, you're not empowered to help yourself. I had a lot of what I needed; I just didn't realise it.'

Benazir Bhutto

Politician
21 June 1953 – 27 December 2007
Pakistan

Benazir Bhutto was a Pakistani politician who became Prime Minister of Pakistan, elected to serve two terms: 1988 to 1990, and again from 1993 to 1996. She was the first woman in a Muslim majority nation to lead a democratic government.

Bhutto was born in Karachi into a wealthy and influential family and had a privileged upbringing. She was close to her father, Pakistan's prime minister from 1973 to 1977, and learned a great deal from him. Confident, graceful and brilliant, Benazir wanted to follow in her father's footsteps and help her own country progress. She pursued higher education at Harvard and Oxford Universities. As a student, she was interested in movements advocating for social justice and political change. After completing her studies, she returned to Pakistan and saw her father re-elected; but a military coup soon ensued, and he was ousted, arrested on allegations of ordering a political assassination, and later executed. The trial was widely condemned, but by then the country was under Mohammed Zia ul-Haq's dictatorship, where it would remain for over a decade, until he died in a plane crash in 1988.

Bhutto was devastated by her father's death, but she had learned from him how to stay strong. She refused to flee Pakistan and took to the streets in the form of peaceful protests, where she raised her voice for democracy and against injustice. She was imprisoned or placed under house arrest on many occasions but proved unstoppable. 'Long live Bhutto!' was her refrain, implying that although her father was gone, he and his principles remained alive in the hearts of the people.

After a period of exile, Benazir returned to Pakistan and led her party, the Pakistan Peoples Party, to victory in the 1988 elections. She became the first female prime minister in the Muslim world, serving two non-consecutive terms. In 2007, she was assassinated in Rawalpindi by a suicide bomber at a political rally, where she was campaigning ahead of the January 2008 elections.

Berta Cáceres

Environmental Activist
4 March 1971 – 3 March 2016
Honduras

Berta Cáceres, of the indigenous Lenca people of Honduras, grew up watching her mother – a midwife and congresswoman – help refugees from El Salvador. Cáceres would dedicate her own life to advocating for change in Honduras, where the rights of Indigenous people are routinely violated, activists are killed, and a woman dies every eighteen hours.

In 1993, Cáceres co-founded the Council of Popular and Indigenous Organisations of Honduras (COPINH), which has helped thousands of Indigenous people save their land from privatisation. Sadly, this threat never disappeared, and after the 2009 coup, when corruption, violence and land seizure hit an all-time high in Honduras, people needed the help of COPINH more than ever.

In 2006, Lenca people from the Río Blanco region sought COPINH's help: heavy equipment was being brought into their towns suspiciously, and tractors were destroying farmland. Construction on a major dam on the Gualcarque River was beginning, led by the biggest dam corporation in the world. Cáceres realised this would not be an easy fight. The river is essential for the Lencas' water supply, food and medicinal plants, and is held sacred by them.

Alongside the community, Cáceres designed a grassroots campaign to stop the project, which included letters to the government, installing a proper process for the people to vote on the dam (result: overwhelmingly against); and peaceful protests. After years of resistance, Cáceres organised a blockade in 2013, which lasted for over a year. Protestors were beaten, shot and tortured by the military, which killed community leader Tomás García. News of these human-rights violations discouraged the project's investors: at the end of the year, it was scrapped.

Cáceres's courageous efforts won her the prestigious Goldman Environmental Prize in 2015, and she travelled throughout Asia, Europe and Latin America, speaking on Indigenous rights and environmental preservation. Despite receiving daily death threats, Cáceres did not stop fighting. In 2016, she was assassinated in her home.

Beyoncé Knowles-Carter

Singer and Songwriter
Born 4 September 1981
United States of America

Beyoncé Knowles (her given name pays homage to her mother's surname before marriage), was a shy girl from Houston, Texas. Her natural vocal gifts were first discovered by a teacher. Beyoncé's first singing success happened at a talent show when, aged seven, she won against teenage contestants with her version of John Lennon's 'Imagine'.

Beyoncé and two friends formed a group called Girl's Tyme and became stars of Houston's talent-show circuit. In 1992, they decided to go national, and entered a television talent show. They didn't win, but four years later, after much hard work and sacrifice, the band was signed by Columbia Records as Destiny's Child (a new name based on a Biblical passage). Beyoncé began emerging as a talented songwriter as well.

By the time Destiny's Child disbanded in 2004, it was one of the most successful 'girl groups' in history. Beyoncé had already launched her solo career in 2003, and now turned to it full time. Already accustomed to sold-out venues and performing at events such as the Super Bowl championship (she would later sing at President Barack Obama's inaugurations as well), Beyoncé was on her way to attaining certifiable superstar status. Her artistry and range deepened too during these years, with her creation of alter ego 'Sasha Fierce' (2008) and her most acclaimed work, *Lemonade*. A 'visual album' – the accompanying video incorporates the words of British-Somali poet Warsan Shire – *Lemonade* was hailed as a breakthrough musically, vocally and thematically. The songs work meaningfully with personal, political and social issues, and have a special focus on Black feminism.

With dozens of awards, millions of records sold, philanthropical and activist bona fides, business ventures and a growing legacy as a global cultural icon, 'Queen Bey' is one of the most singular artists of the twenty-first century.

Calypso Rose

Singer and Songwriter
Born 27 April 1940
Trinidad and Tobago

Linda McCartha Monica Sandy-Lewis grew up with a speech impediment. When she was nine, her aunt and uncle adopted her. Her aunt had many records, and would play them and dance with her niece, introducing her to calypso music – a music form rooted in traditions developed by West African slaves brought to the Caribbean – and helping her to overcome her speech difficulties. Rose's own grandmother was originally from French Guinea, but was kidnapped and sold, ending up in Tobago.

As a teenager in 1955, Rose composed her first song, Glass Thief, and auditioned in front of the managers to sing in a calypso tent called Young Brigade. The managers gave her the name 'Calypso Rose', which she immediately adopted.

Rose was not the first female calypsonian, but the field was so male-dominated that Trinidad's prestigious calypso competition recognised the winner as 'Calypso King' of the year. Rose became the first woman to win the title in 1978, and the title was changed to 'Calypso Monarch' in her honour. She was also the first woman to win the celebrated Road March award in Trinidad in 1977. She is now by far the most recognised female Calypso singer and is considered the 'mother of calypso'.

Over her six-decade-plus career, Calypso Rose has written more than 800 songs, won a number of awards and honours and spread calypso music from Trinidad and Tobago to the rest of the world. Her songs often address women's issues such as violence, harassment and infidelity; encouraging women to stand up for and respect themselves. Her 2016 song 'Leave Me Alone' inspired a Twitter campaign (#LeaveSheAlone) and became a women's-rights anthem at the Trinidad and Tobago Carnival. In 2012, aged 72, she revealed that she had been married to a woman for seventeen years.

Calypso prevailed over cancer twice, in 1996 and several years later. The ordeals made her believe she had been spared for specific reasons: to unite people, and to make them joyful through music.

Claudia Jones

Journalist and Activist
21 February 1915 – 24 December 1964
United States of America and United Kingdom

Claudia Vera Cumberbatch was born in Trinidad, raised in the US and later became a British citizen. A steadfast advocate of communism, feminism and Black nationalism, she was also the founder of London's world-famous Notting Hill Carnival.

Jones (she assumed this surname early on) was a bright, impoverished teenager who, convalescing from tuberculosis, read widely on social issues and inequality. She joined the Communist Party and the Young Communist League in the US, occupying key positions in both by 1946. Jones distinguished herself on national committees, as an editor of communist newspapers and as a writer. Her 1949 essay 'An End to the Neglect of the Problems of Negro Women' is often cited as an early work on what is now termed intersectionality.

Jones was arrested and incarcerated for her political activities, and her health worsened. In 1955, US authorities attempted to deport her to Trinidad and Tobago, who refused to receive her. However, Britain offered her asylum, and Jones arrived in London as the British-Caribbean community was growing – the result of the post-war influx of Caribbean immigrants. Jones quickly got to work organising her new community, campaigning against racism and discrimination, raising consciousness and – in 1958 – founding *The West Indian Gazette and Afro-Asian Caribbean News*, Britain's first major Black newspaper and a seminal forum for the Caribbean diaspora.

In 1959, Jones created the Notting Hill Carnival, after the murder of an Antiguan expatriate by white extremists ignited riots in London. The Carnival is now one of the largest in the world, attended by millions each year in a show of strength and solidarity with Caribbean communities.

Jones was widely recognised for her activism, forming relationships with luminaries such as Paul Robeson and Martin Luther King, Jr, and speaking publicly in Japan, the USSR and China. She died of heart failure at forty-nine, her contributions to her community and to the wider community of humankind hugely disproportional to her short lifespan.

Clemantine Wamariya

Storyteller and Human Rights Activist
Born 18 December 1988
Rwanda

Clemantine Wamariya's happy early childhood was shattered in April 1994 when the Rwandan genocide began. More than 800,000 people, mainly of the Tutsi ethnic group, were murdered in just over three months. As violence broke out, Wamariya's Tutsi parents sent her, with her older sister Claire, to presumed safety at their grandmother's farm. However, days later, the armed militia *génocidaires* came knocking. Wamariya's grandmother told the girls to flee. No one else survived that knock.

Led by Claire, the sisters sought refuge in seven countries over six years, passing through Burundi, Zaire, Tanzania, Malawi, Mozambique, South Africa and Zambia before being granted asylum in the US in 2000. Clementine lived with a family in Chicago and attended high school; Claire, now a mother herself, lived nearby and had a cleaning job.

In 2006, Clementine submitted an essay on Elie Wiesel's Holocaust memoir, *Night,* for a National High School Essay Contest sponsored by television host, Oprah Winfrey. If Rwandans had read it, she posited, they might not have killed one another. She won the competition and was invited to appear on *The Oprah Winfrey Show* with Claire. The girls were shocked by the surprise appearance of their parents there: Winfrey had had them flown over from Rwanda. The girls knew they had survived but had not seen them for twelve years.

Wamariya went on to study comparative literature at Yale University and wrote a memoir. She spoke widely for the United States Holocaust Memorial Museum and was later appointed to its board by Barack Obama. She now works as a human rights advocate, fighting for the unprivileged and championing justice.

'Every American ... who wants to know what hate can do should look at what happened in Rwanda,' she has said. 'If you want to know that peace is possible, you should also look at Rwanda now.'

Deepika Padukone

Actress and Mental Health Advocate
Born 5 January 1986
India

Deepika Padukone was born in Denmark before moving to India with her family at the age of one. Her father was a professional badminton player, and Deepika proved adept at it as well, playing to national level. Badminton seemed to be her destiny, but in college she was spotted and recruited as a model. Shortly afterwards, Bollywood beckoned.

In 2007, Padukone made her debut as a lead actress in a commercially successful film. Padukone became a star. Her films were blockbusters; her fans were counted in the millions; she won awards; and every filmmaker in the industry wanted to work with her. One of the biggest names in Bollywood, she would also later work in Hollywood. Despite these incredible career successes, one morning in 2014 she woke up and her world was a few shades darker. She felt as though everything was falling apart. A few weeks later, she realised she was suffering from depression and her mother encouraged her to seek medical help. As Padukone was researching depression and trying to find out what was happening to her, she came to see how little information was available about mental health. Resources available to people with mental health illnesses were few and far between. These experiences showed her that in India, heavy stigma remains around mental health issues and people are subsequently unwilling to talk about them.

In 2015, even as Padukone continued to deal with depression, she decided to help others. She started to speak out about her own mental health, and set up a foundation called Live, Love Laugh, through which she set up various resources for people seeking information and aid. Padukone wanted more attention paid to mental illness and its effects – and less shame to be associated with it.

Today, Padukone is a brighter star of Bollywood than ever before and continues to advocate for better mental health support.

Elif Shafak

Author
Born 25 October 1971
Turkey

Elif Shafak was born in Strasbourg, France. After her parents' divorce, she moved to Ankara, Turkey, with her mother. Growing up, she would observe her mother, a strong, well-educated, Westernised woman, and also her grandmother – traditional, superstitious and minimally educated. Shafak loved how these two women, who were so different, coexisted beautifully. Their relationship had a great impact on her as a person and, later, as a writer.

An introverted child, Shafak told stories to her imaginary friends. Her mother suggested she keep a journal in which to express them, but Shafak didn't want to write about herself; she preferred stories about things that didn't exist. Thus, at the age of eight, she began writing fiction.

When her mother became a diplomat, they moved to Spain, and Shafak attended an international school. There, she observed students from troubled countries being mocked and bullied. This also happened to her when Turkey's difficulties were in the news. That people could see not her, but only the country she came from, was a shock. As an adult, Shafak saw these behaviours grow into damaging stereotypes. She often heard women in Europe or the US express gratitude that they hadn't been born in the 'oppressive' Middle East. Similarly, in the Middle East, she met women who were grateful not to have been born in the 'over-sexualised' West. Unfamiliar with each other's stories, they had nevertheless categorised their respective origins as undesirable. Through her writing – seventeen books to date, translated into fifty languages – Shafak builds bridges and cuts through boundaries. Her themes include women's lives, immigration, culture and much more that is close to her heart.

Shafak believes that storytelling has power to change the world. One of the most-read authors in Turkey, she has won many prestigious awards, including the Chevalier de l'Ordre des Arts et des Lettres, and has twice been a TED Global speaker. Her beliefs and work also go beyond the page and she is a passionate supporter for the rights of minorities and women, and freedom of expression.

Esra'a Al Shafei

Human Rights Activist
Born 23 July 1989
Bahrain

Growing up, Esra'a observed the mistreatment of migrant workers in Bahrain. She wanted to discuss this, and other political and social issues; but her family, peers and teachers discouraged her. Esra'a experienced anxiety and depression at not being able to express herself.

At fourteen, Esra'a would spend hours in the school library, using the internet to learn about different cultures and values. At fifteen, she envisioned a platform where people could express themselves and their opinions without fearing backlash. At twenty, she registered Majal.org (Mideast Youth) officially, and a platform was born that, over the following years, amplified marginalised voices in the region. Esra'a invited hundreds of authors from across the Middle East and North Africa to write about diversity, activism, freedom of speech, human rights and more. It also grew numerous offshoot sub-platforms, with Majal.org at the heart of the hub. In 2010, for example, Esra'a created Mideast Tunes, the largest platform in the region for underground musicians who use music to fight social injustice.

For many years, Al Shafei was unable to register her platform as a non-profit organisation, and could not apply for grants, so she worked part-time as a tech consultant and built websites, investing her earnings in Majal. Al Shafei did not study computer science at university: her skills in the field are self-taught.

Al Shafei keeps a low profile. She avoids posting photos of herself and her face is not shown in interviews or recordings of her speeches. These are safety precautions; many activists in her field have been imprisoned, tortured, killed or exiled. Although the world may not know her face, Al Shafei has been recognised around the world as an innovator and social entrepreneur. She has appeared on lists including BBC 100 Women and Forbes magazine's 30 Under 30, has been a senior TED Fellow and a Director's Fellow at MIT Media Lab, and won many awards. Hers is a life dedicated to bringing about change.

Esther Afua Ocloo

Entrepreneur
18 April 1919 – 8 February 2002
Ghana

In the 1930s a teenager named Esther Afua Nkulenu started selling her homemade marmalade. Her schoolmates made fun of her at the time for being a common street vendor, but this was the beginning of an inspiring entrepreneurial journey for African women.

Esther Afua Ocloo's (née Esther Afua Nkulenu) parents had little, but they made sure their daughter received an education when she was young. Esther then won a scholarship to study at the prestigious Achimota School in Accra. Although her better-off peers mocked Ocloo for her traditional clothing and accent and she had difficulty fitting in, she persisted with her studies.

After graduation, using her pocket money, Ocloo bought the ingredients to make that now-legendary marmalade. As business picked up, she signed contracts with the Achimota School and later the military to supply them with her product. She then obtained a bank loan, and in 1942 established Nkulenu Industries, Ghana's first food-processing company.

The school sponsored Ocloo's further education abroad, at the Good Housekeeping Institute in London. She became its first African graduate, and later enrolled at Bristol University to study food preservation techniques. When she returned to Ghana, her company began producing canned foods. Ocloo also set up training programmes for women who wanted to start their own businesses.

In 1975, at the UN's first-ever World Conference on Women, Ocloo declared that, although Ghanaian women were entrepreneurial by nature, banks weren't willing to finance them. A few years later, alongside Ela Bhatt and Michaela Walsh – two women she had met at the conference – she co-founded Women's World Banking. WWB has since funded over 16 million women around the globe. Ocloo is thus a pioneer of microlending and a strong advocate of women's financial liberation.

In 1990, she became the first woman to receive the Africa Prize for Leadership. Today, among other food exports, Nkulenu Industries still makes marmalade.

Esther Mahlangu

Artist
Born 11 November 1935
South Africa

Esther Mahlangu was ten when she began imitating her mother and her grandmother, who filled the exteriors of their mud-walled house with traditional Ndebele mural designs. When they rested from painting in the hot sun, young Esther would pick up the chicken feathers they used as brushes and resume where they had left off. Upon their return, she would get into trouble: her lines weren't straight, and she lacked training in the style.

She loved the form, however, and being scolded didn't stop her from painting daily. The older women relented, allowing her to paint the back of the house. Her lines eventually became straighter, and her designs grew beautiful. Finally, she was given the front walls to paint.

As Mahlangu grew older, her devotion to Ndebele art deepened. She became an expert at painting murals. To obtain white, black, red, yellow and green, she used soil, clay, cow dung, limestone, ash and water – mixtures so strong that rainstorms can't wash the colours away.

When French art researchers came to Mahlangu's village and learned of her work, they invited her to participate in an art exhibition, 'Magicians of the World', in France. Thus Mahlangu's work became widely known. In 1991 she became the first woman to participate in the prestigious BMW Art Car Project, painting Ndebele designs.

Mahlangu's art now features in collections worldwide, and she loves to travel – always in traditional clothing – and share her culture and heritage. Voicing concerns that young Africans are becoming detached from their roots, she has said '... If the young children don't learn from the elders, then everything will vanish.' To that end Mahlangu started a school in her backyard, training girls to make Ndebele art, so that they, in turn, could teach subsequent generations. In her own actions, and words, Mahlangu is true to her belief that 'no culture must come to an end.'

Fairuz

Singer
Born 21 November 1935
Lebanon

'The Lebanese,' a popular expression goes, 'disagree about everything – except Fairuz.' Indeed, Nouhad al-Haddad (who adopted the stage name 'Fairuz' ['Turquoise'] in the 1950s) is not only a Lebanese icon; she is also revered as one of the world's great divas.

Young Nouhad's family was unable to afford a radio, but she used to listen to their neighbour's, and imitate the songs she overheard. One day, when she was ten years old, a musician who taught at the Conservatory heard her singing as part of her school choir. He advised her to enrol in the Conservatory. She was successful.

One of Fairuz's first breakthroughs came when she was hired by Radio Lebanon as a chorus singer. Here, she met the Rahbani brothers, who were innovative musicians and composers. They began collaborating with Fairuz and it was a magical union from the beginning. Fairuz was quickly establihed as one of the Arab world's most outstanding performers. Fairuz's partnership with brother Assi Rahbani, who composed her songs, also grew, and they eventually married.

In the 1960s, Fairuz and the Rahbanis melded Western and traditional styles in their music, and Fairuz's lyrics became more political, as well. Operettas, radio, film, television, festivals: Fairuz was omnipresent, and her fame multiplied.

In 1975, Lebanon's tragic fifteen-year-long civil war began. Fairuz made music lamenting the bloody violence while refusing to take sides. She did not perform in Lebanon during this time. With the exception of travelling abroad to give concerts, Fairuz and the Rabhani brothers never left the country, as vast numbers of Lebanese – understandably – did. Fairuz became a symbol of Lebanese unity and was beloved by all sides. When Assi Rahbani died in 1986, a ceasefire was declared to allow the widowed singer to bury her husband.

Fairuz continues to perform to this day. The recipient of numerous honours worldwide she continues to be an enigmatic, commanding presence on stage – and the most-listened-to singer in the Arab world.

Fatema Mernissi

Sociologist and Feminist
7 September 1940 – 30 November 2015
Morocco

_____

'The male elite faction is trying to convince us that their egoistic, highly subjective and mediocre view of culture and society has a sacred basis,' Fatema Mernissi wrote in 1991. A leading advocate for women's writes in the Muslim world, today she is considered one of the founders of Islamic feminism.

Born in Fez in 1940, Mernissi grew up in a domestic harem with her mother, grandmother and female members of her extended family. Her grandfather had multiple wives, though her father was monogamous and Mernissi's mother was his only wife. Women were sequestered in such quarters away from male outsiders, but growing up, Mernissi often wondered why this was so.

Mernissi's mother listened covertly to discussions about nationalism and forward-looking Arab movements on the radio, and hated her confined life. Fortunately for Mernissi, she came of age during a progressive moment and had the opportunity to step outside the harem doors and receive an education, unlike her mother. She studied at Mohammed V University in Rabat and the Sorbonne in Paris, and ultimately obtained a PhD from Brandeis University in the US. Her important first book, *Beyond the Veil: Male–Female Dynamics in Muslim Society*, was adapted from her dissertation.

Eventually, Mernissi returned to Morocco and began a career teaching at Mohammad V University. Her thorough research explored women in Islamic history as well as behaviours in present-day society, demonstrating that they had had equal rights, decision-making power and freedom. She was then able to show in her vigorous work how Islam and the Qur'an had been deliberately misinterpreted by men for centuries, to their own benefit. Her many brilliant, essential texts on women and Islam are widely read today and her writing has been translated in thirty different languages. In 2003, along with Susan Sontag, she received Spain's prestigious Prince of Asturias Award for Letters.

Fatima al-Fihri

Pioneering Educator
Early 800 – 880 CE
Tunisia

While ninth-century queens and empresses had some say in political, trade and personal matters, self-determination was a luxury for ordinary and even wealthy women. They lived within many limitations and had little control over decision-making outside the spheres of household work, wifehood and motherhood. Fatima al-Fihri was an exception to this rule.

Fatima al-Fihri was born in the city of al-Qayrawan, in present-day Tunisia. Her father was a rich merchant. During the rule of Idris II, her family – like many other Arab families – migrated to Fez, in present-day Morocco. They valued learning and made sure that Fatima and her sister received the best education possible. Fatima inherited those values, as well as building philanthropic ones of her own. She gave to charity frequently and also mentored other students.

When both al-Fihri's father and husband died, she inherited great wealth. She recognised the growing Muslim community's need for a mosque in Fez and decided to turn this into a reality. Around 859 CE, she invested her money to build one that could hold over 20,000 worshipers; it remains among the biggest in Africa today, over a thousand years later. Al-Fihri ensured that it contained classrooms and a library.

Later, al-Fihri also founded what is now the University of al-Qarawiyyin, which takes its name from her hometown. It is the oldest continuously operating institution of higher learning in the world and was the first to award degrees to students. Records show that its library held thousands of precious titles, and Fatima made sure that the curriculum of the institution included Qur'anic studies, Mathematics, Medicine, Music, Astronomy and various other subjects. Students from around the known world have been educated there, including great scientists, doctors and visionaries such as Leo Africanus, Nicolas Cleynaerts, Ibn Khaldun, Maimonides and Ibn Rushd.

These legacies were how al-Fihri was able to thank the community that had welcomed her and her family. She was a true pioneer of the higher education system; a woman who educated the world.

Faye Simanjuntak

Human Rights Activist
Born 10 April 2002
Indonesia

As a child, Faye Simanjuntak lived a regular life surrounded by friends and family. Her parents emphasised the importance of giving back to the community to her as she was growing up, regularly taking Faye to visit orphanages, which she didn't enjoy: she'd have preferred to hang out with her friends.

Her attitude changed when her mother took her on a seven-day trip to visit ten orphanages. Faye got a deeper look at the lives of those orphans and the staff working there. It was life-altering. When she returned home, she spoke to her mother about helping the children more. Faye decided to write over a hundred letters to friends and family, requesting them to donate money for the orphanages instead of buying her birthday gifts that year. Faye thought she would be able to raise 1 million Indonesian rupiah which is approximately £50 or $65. To her surprise, she raised over Rp 96 million. Faye felt that she needed to do more. While she was brainstorming ideas, she learned about social injustice at school. She was shocked to find out about trafficking, realising that this dark world that wasn't limited to adults, but that children were victimised as well. She thought, 'Surely this doesn't happen in Indonesia.' She did some research and was devastated to learn that hundreds and thousands of children were trafficked every year in her home country. Later, she met a girl who was married at ten, became a mother at eleven and was trafficked at twelve.

Faye began to take action. Aged twelve, she started an organisation, Rumah Faye, to help victims of child trafficking. Her organisation provided those in need – some who had been forced into child labour and prostitution – with resources for recovery and supporting programmes to help them get back on their feet. Simanjuntak has shown that no one is too young to make a difference. Since the organisation began, she has helped rescue over ninety girls and five babies in her mission to fight child trafficking.

Felícitas Méndez

Activist
5 February 1916 – 12 April 1998
Puerto Rico

Years before the landmark *Brown v. Board of Education* ruling in the US that spelled the end of racial school segregation, a young Hispanic couple defied prejudice, fought for integration – and won.

Felícitas Gómez had encountered racism and ignorance since moving with her family from Puerto Rico to the mainland US in 1926, to work as agricultural labourers. But there were also opportunities: in 1936, she married Gonzalo Méndez, and the couple leased a farm in Westminster, Orange County (its Japanese-American owners had been sent to World War II internment camps) and opened a bar and grill.

In 1944, the couple attempted to enrol their three children at a local school that provided a demonstrably better education than the two-room, wooden-shack school the children attended. In keeping with segregation policies that operated across much of the US, they were refused by the explicitly 'whites-only' school. The school contrived various dishonest reasons for declining the children, including hygiene and language issues.

The Méndezes decided to take legal action. Gonzalo banded together with four other Hispanic fathers, devoting themselves to *Méndez v. Westminster*, a class-action suit against several school districts. Felícitas organised support committees within the community, while also single-handedly (and very profitably) managing the farm. In 1946, a federal district court ruled that the Hispanic families turned away by the schools had been denied 'equal protection under the law' – the basis of the Fourteenth Amendment of the US Constitution. The ruling was upheld on appeal, and applied to the state as a whole; in fact, it set the scene for the *Brown* decision in 1954.

At first, the school offered a settlement only to the Méndezes, to avoid committing to any permanent change in their system. The couple refused and continued to campaign for wider desegregation in schools. Felícitas later told her daughter: 'When we decided to fight, it was not only for you, but for all the children.'

Frida Kahlo

Artist
6 July 1907 – 13 July 1954
Mexico

The name of Frida Kahlo – like her style, one of the most recognisable in modern art – summons many associations: passionate intensity, pain and joy, the search for self in enigmatic, singular works. Pain would, in fact, be her constant companion, but she confronted it in her art.

Kahlo grew up in a loving home known as *'la Casa Azul'* ('the Blue House'). Left with a withered leg from polio at nine, she hid it by wearing long skirts characteristic of the Tehuana women of southern Mexico – a choice determined by her attraction to Indigenous traditions, and to symbols of female power (Tehuanas are known for their independence).

When she was eighteen, Kahlo was involved in a wrenching bus accident which left her with serious injuries. The damage her body sustained also left her unable to bear children – another harsh consequence of the trauma she had endured. She was confined to bed for a long convalescence. Her parents built an easel that hung overhead, enabling her to paint sitting up.

Kahlo painted mostly self-portraits evoking her struggles. 'I paint myself because I am often alone,' she said, 'and I am the subject I know best.' André Breton, the chief proponent of Surrealism, declared her a Surrealist painter, but she would not call herself that: Kahlo believed she painted her reality.

Although she often felt overshadowed by her husband Diego Rivera, the more famous artist (then, if not nowadays), people responded strongly to the intimate power of her paintings, as well as to Kahlo's own power. She exhibited around the world, with her first Mexican solo show occurring in 1953. By then her health had declined, and she had little mobility; nevertheless, she attended the opening in an ambulance and stayed for the evening, propped up on a gurney.

Today, the *Casa Azul* is a museum, and Kahlo's legacy as a vital artist and vibrant feminist icon lives on.

Funmilayo Ransome-Kuti

Women's Rights Activist
25 October 1900 – 13 April 1978
Nigeria

Frances Abigail Olufunmilayo Thomas (who later de-Anglicised her name to reflect her Yoruba roots) is synonymous with the establishment of women's rights in Nigeria. The daughter of a chief who believed in girls' education, she was the first female grammar-school student in Abeokuta, capital of Ogun State. She then went to England where she attended a finishing school, before returning to Nigeria and marrying the notable educator Israel Ransome-Kuti. The couple had a loving, respectful and equitable relationship until his death three decades later.

Throughout her life, Ransome-Kuti worked to liberate women. In the 1930s, she organised literacy classes for female market workers in Abeokuta. In 1944 she mounted a successful defence of these destitute, exploited women against predatory official practices and price controls. The regional movement she headed admitted women of all classes, and promoted Yoruba customs. In 1946 she protested discriminatory taxing and harassment by the British-backed local potentate, and campaigned for better sanitation, education, healthcare and social services. Public sympathy grew, as did Ransome-Kuti's pressure tactics, until the policies ended and women became more empowered.

Ransome-Kuti went on to create the Nigerian Women's Union, with branches across the country. Its main objectives were full representation and greater decision-making power for women at the highest levels. A figure of national prominence, she was also invited to speak abroad, including at a notable London conference on the Nigerian constitution, where she was the only female delegate from her country. There, she criticised colonial rule and lobbied for women's suffrage. Subject to a travel ban and threatened with arrest after speaking in the USSR and China, she ran for federal office, unsuccessfully. However, she remained a political force, as fearless in her criticism of corrupt authority both before and after Nigera's independence.

In 1977, soldiers of Nigeria's military government marauded a Lagos compound where Ransome-Kuti was visiting her son, the infamous dissident-musician Fela, who lived there. Ransome-Kuti was thrown out a window and died from her injuries – a profoundly sad ending to a life that had influenced millions.

Germaine Acogny

Dancer, Choreographer, Teacher
Born 28 May 1944
Senegal

The major figure in contemporary African dance, Germaine Acogny pioneers performances that 'reflect Africa today, an Africa of skyscrapers, an Africa of great international contradictions'. Born in Benin and raised in Senegal, dance has taken Acogny around the world. Her formative training took place in Paris and Brussels with one of the world's top dance directors, Maurice Béjart, at his school, Mudra. She continues to be celebrated far and wide today.

Supported in her work, travels and studies by Senegal's poet-president Léopold Sédar Senghor, Acogny returned to Sengal in 1968 and opened a studio in Dakar. From 1977–82, she was the Director of Mudra Afrique, in collaboration with Béjart and the Senghor government. Twenty years later, after redefining African dance and becoming one of the world's most electric and innovative performers, she opened the École des Sables – a seminal centre for contemporary African choreography.

Through her dances and teachings, Acogny has reframed African dance for the ages. With roots in traditional forms, her philosophy is to 'respect the body without distorting it'. Her training in ballet and Modern European dance continues to inform her work, which is visceral, strenuous, kinetically and emotionally charged. Acogny combines highly original, typical movements with powerful bursts of shouts and laughter, marching and running. Her performances confront patriarchy, colonialism and injustice, and also celebrate nature and transcendence. As well as expressing herself through dance, Acogny has also written; her book *African Dance* (1980) assails common biases (for example, that there is no 'technique' involved in African dance), details African dance's complexity as an artform, and advances its traditional movement into the twentieth century.

Acogny has created many original and famous solo and company works, was awarded Chevalier de l'Ordre du Mérite and Officier de l'Ordre des Arts et des Lettres by France and Chevalier de l'Ordre National du Lion by Senegal and collaborated with some of the finest choreographers and performers over decades. Now in her seventies, she still dances, and continues to rehearse new works.

Guo Jianmei

Women's Rights Lawyer
Born 13 October 1961
China

Guo Jianmei was born into a peasant family in Henan Province, and grew up hearing stories of women suffering patriarchal injustice. Her grandmother was humiliated and divorced by her grandfather for bearing only daughters; her other grandmother starved to death, too scared of her husband to avail herself of the steamed buns she sold at the market after the men took their share.

As a young girl in Beijing, Guo was bullied for her accent and peasant origins. Such experiences helped her build up a store of empathy that would serve her well.

Guo gained admission to Peking University Law School and worked at the Ministry of Justice after graduation. In 1995, she attended the Fourth World Conference on Women in Beijing. She arrived at the conference in order to observe and interview the women who were participating, but after joining the discussions about the violation of women's rights in China, Guo left as an activist. She quit her job and co-founded a non-profit organisation that became the Zhongze Women's Legal Counselling Service Centre.

The centre helped disadvantaged women, victims of domestic violence, sexual harassment and gender discrimination, learn their rights and protect themselves. Guo's early battles were not easy. The justice system did not favour women, and she lost many cases. She suffered depression and anxiety – but never stopped advocating for her clients. The work was fulfilling; it was their circumstances that devastated her.

For twenty-one years, the centre provided free legal assistance to over 100,000 women and brought 4,000 lawsuits. Guo's efforts, alongside those of other activists, saw China's first law against domestic violence passed in 2016. However, Guo and her allies have endured much aggression from Chinese society, and the government shut down the centre in 2016. Despite this, Guo continues her work as China's first public-interest lawyer fighting full-time on the frontlines to protect women's rights.

Hanan Ashrawi

Political Leader, Activist and Scholar
Born 8 October 1946
Palestine

Hanan Ashrawi is a prominent voice for peace and civil society. She has been, arguably, the most pragmatic, clear-headed and unimpeachable figure involved in the so-called Middle East peace process – the decades-long attempt to establish an independent Palestinian state. A steadfast advocate of the two-state solution, she has been Palestine's most visible spokesperson in the West.

Like many Palestinians, Ashrawi's family fled to Jordan in 1948. They later returned to Palestine and settled in Ramallah. Ashrawi's father, a founder of the Palestine Liberation Organisation (PLO), nurtured his daughter's critical thinking and activist spirit. During the 1967 war, when Ashrawi was studying in Beirut, she was denied re-entry into Palestine. Instead, she went to the US and earn her PhD, returning to Palestine in 1973 to take up a position at Birzeit University.

During the First Intifada in 1987, Ashrawi became an eloquent and passionate commentator on US television news. Her political profile grew, and she became a senior (and the first female) member of the Executive Committee of the PLO – effectively, the government of Palestine. As part of her role, she negotiated with the US over the specifics of Palestinian participation at the 1991–93 peace talks in Madrid and Washington. She also served on legislative and communications committees, as education minister and as one of the leaders of the Third Way centrist party. She resigned from the PLO in 2020, protesting the organisation's cooperation with Israel after the latter announced plans for another annexation of part of occupied Palestine.

Ashrawi has proven herself one of the most astute participant-observers of the history of Palestine since 1948, and a tireless advocate for justice and freedom. A vigorous activist for civil society, she has established foundations and commissions for global dialogue and democracy, accountability, integrity and human rights.

Hayat Sindi

Scientist and Social Entrepreneur
Born 6 November 1967
Saudi Arabia

Hayat Sindi, born in Makkah, Saudi Arabia, is one of the world's leading biotech scientists and has achieved many 'firsts' for women in the country. One of the first women to sit on the Saudi Consultative Council, an important advisory body to the monarch, she was also the first Saudi woman to gain admission to Cambridge University's Biotechnology programme and the first Gulf Arab woman to obtain a doctorate in the field.

'Being a woman,' she has said, 'meant [earning] the respect of colleagues.' She has also spoken of the prejudices that she has had to overcome to earn that respect, for example, that her 'choice to wear the headscarf was inconsistent' with her 'choice to study a natural science.'

Sindi had the support of her parents in pursuing her passion for science. She arrived in London, quickly learned English and obtained a degree at King's College in Pharmacology, winning a prize there for her work on allergies. Facing down doubt and criticism, she moved on to Cambridge and into prominence, later becoming a Visiting Scholar at Harvard University. Sindi maintains a key interest in furthering science education generally and among women, and in further developing Saudi scientific research. She founded the i2 Institute for Imaginative Ingenuity in Riyadh to foster 'an ecosystem of entrepreneurship and social innovation for scientists, technologists and engineers in the Middle East and beyond'.

Another part of Sindi's ground-breaking work includes her role as co-founder of Diagnostics for All. Diagnostics for All is a non-profit enterprise that works on innovations which require neither medical expertise nor electricity, meaning they can be rolled out fairly cheaply to those who need them most. These innovations are used most in the developing world. Sindi's own inventions for Diagnostics for All include a Magnetic Acoustic Resonance Sensor, which help diagnose illnesses on the spot – invaluable in places where advanced healthcare is scarce.

Heidy Quah

Human Rights Activist
Born 21 May 1994
Malaysia

Refuge for the Refugees, as a name for an organisation, might seem redundant at first. In Malaysia, however, refugees are not recognised by the government: the country is not a signatory to the 1951 UN Refugee Convention. Refugee children cannot obtain schooling; nor are families provided with housing.

In 2012, after completing her secondary school education, Heidy Quah worked for four months as an English teacher at a school for Burmese refugees in Kuala Lumpur. As she prepared to leave her post to study full-time for a Business degree, she was informed that the school would be shutting down from lack of funding. Quah was moved to action. She and her friend Andrea Prisha raised funds by selling cookies and working social media; within a week, they brought in enough to maintain the school for another few months.

Shortly afterwards, Quah – facing down criticism and indifference – co-founded Refuge for the Refugees as a non-profit organisation and 'a voice for the voiceless'. She was eighteen years old.

'Realising there are children out there who don't have what I would consider basic necessities ... man, that was really difficult,' Quah has said. 'I was so shaken by how messed up the world is. I carried so much shame and guilt at my own privilege ... But then I reframed that and thought ... "Instead of stewing in guilt, how could I channel it positively"?'

Today, Refuge for the Refugees supports several dozen schools in Malaysia and Myanmar, which care for 2,000 children. It connects schools with resources such as volunteer teachers, syllabus development and fundraising, and helps vulnerable refugees at risk of exploitation and mistreatment to acquire confidence and pursue better lives. It also spreads awareness about their status in Malaysia.

Quah continues to draw attention to the difficulties refugees face today, and has spoken and conducted training at more than 100 events worldwide.

Ibtihaj Muhammad

Fencer
Born 4 December 1984
United States of America

In Ibtihaj Muhammad's family, playing sports was simply what you did: her brother played football; her sister, volleyball; and Muhammad herself grew up playing softball and tennis, and running track.

Muhammad is Muslim and wears a hijab. Her mother, recognising that sports made her daughter happy, never wanted her to encounter any kind of barriers. She altered her sports uniforms by adding longer sleeves or extending the legs on shorts, so that Muhammad would feel comfortable without needing to compromise her preferred style of dress.

One day, when Muhammad was twelve and riding in a car with her mother, they noticed some masked athletes covered head to toe, sparring with foils: this was her introduction to fencing. Initially, she didn't think much of it, but later she developed a passion for the sport in high school and joined the fencing team. It was the first time Muhammad and her sporting teammates all appeared the same way; her mother didn't have to alter this uniform. She felt that the fencing suit was like armour, conferring superpowers.

Muhammad was highly skilled and led her high school team to two national championships as captain. She continued to excel in the sport at Duke University, began training with a former Olympian in 2009 and won her first national title that same year. Breaking stereotypes and winning numerous medals and accolades – including Muslim Sportswoman of the Year in 2012 – Muhammad earned a spot on the US Olympic fencing team in 2016.

Now a worldwide symbol, Muhammad hadn't realised previously that so many people regarded Muslim women as oppressed and weak. She relished the opportunity to represent them – along with all women of colour – in a different, more positive light. As she said: 'It's not just to challenge misconceptions outside the Muslim community, but within the Muslim community. I want to break cultural norms.'

Muhammad made history when she took the bronze, becoming the first female Muslim-American athlete to win an Olympic medal.

Isabel Allende

Author
Born 2 August 1942
Chile, United States of America

Isabel Allende is a celebrated author of around two dozen works of fiction and non-fiction, including memoirs, short stories and children's books. Her concerns as a writer include feminism, social justice and history, and her writing is known for touches of magical realism.

Born in Peru to Chilean parents, raised in Chile and now a long-time US resident, Allende was inspired to write fiction after interviewing Pablo Neruda as a journalist. Apparently, the great poet disparaged her journalism skills, but praised her storytelling ability, saying she would make a much better novelist.

In 1973, during the military coup in Chile that led directly to the suicide of her cousin Salvador Allende – the country's president – Isabel arranged safe passage for endangered Chileans, then fled to Venezuela. She lived there for thirteen years. During this time, she wrote her most famous novel, *The House of the Spirits*, which began as a letter to her 100-year-old grandfather back in Chile, who was dying.

Allende, one of the world's most widely-read authors, has been published in at least thirty-five languages. Her books have sold approximately 70 million copies. She is also one of the world's most acclaimed writers, having garnered a number of awards and honours including the Presidential Medal of Freedom (US), the Ordre des Arts et des Lettres (France) and the Premio Nacional de Literatura (Chile).

In 1996, she established the Isabel Allende Foundation as a tribute to her daughter, who had died in 1992 on account of a hospital mishap while being treated for a disease. The foundation 'invest[s] in the power of women and girls to secure reproductive rights, economic independence and freedom from violence', and administers grants 'in support of programmes located predominantly in Chile and California, the two regions closest to [Allende's] heart'.

Jaha Dukureh

Women's Rights Activist
Born 1989
The Gambia and United States of America

The movement to end the horrific practice of female genital mutilation (FGM) can claim Jaha Dukureh as a leading figure. Outspoken, frank and deftly able to negotiate hostility from communities that believe in FGM, Dukureh was instrumental in the Gambian ban on the practice. A regular spokesperson on the topic across Africa and the US, she is a UN Women Goodwill Ambassador for Africa and 2018 Nobel Peace Prize nominee.

When she was just one week old, Dukureh became a victim of FGM Type III: the removal of all external genitalia and the sewing together of the wound. FGM is an ancient tradition, performed for reasons of perceived honour, purity, beauty and belonging – and enforced chastity. An estimated 4 million girls are cut every year. It occurs primarily in Africa and Asia as well as in some immigrant communities in the West.

At fifteen, Dukureh was sent to the US to marry a stranger twice her age. She only discovered she had been subjected to FGM when – after sex with the man proved impossible – she went to a clinic to have her sewn labia cut through. When the marriage failed, Dukureh, still a teenager, supported herself and was able to enrol herself in formal education at a New York City high school after many institutions had rejected her. She entered a second arranged marriage, by consent, and now lives happily in Atlanta with her husband and their two children. Dukureh began speaking out against FGM on her blog, then founded the anti-FGM non-profit organisation, Safe Hands for Girls. In 2014, she launched a petition on change.org, asking President Barack Obama to investigate FGM in the US. After the petition collected over 200,000 signatures, the administration took action and Dukureh's journey as a force for change began.

'I ... knew there were millions of girls out there,' she said, '... and no one was speaking for them. If it wasn't going to me, who else would do that?'

Jameela Jamil

Actress
Born 25 February 1986
United Kingdom

Jameela Jamil may be a beautiful woman – but she wants us to think carefully about what we mean when we say that. The British-born former model, radio and television presenter and actress (who was a cast member of the hit US television comedy *The Good Place*) regularly condemns the use of airbrushing to make women look 'perfect'. Jamil will not permit photos of herself to be altered and frequently calls out journalists for making degrading comments about women's looks, as well as other celebrities for marketing appetite suppressants or behaving aggressively toward women.

Jamil is also known for her Instagram account 'I-Weigh', launched in response to the phenomenon of women posting their weight. Instead, the account invites submissions of followers' photos (non-airbrushed, of course), accompanied by the hashtag #iweigh and a description of qualities or accomplishments they are proud of. '["I-Weigh" is] for us to feel valuable ... and look past the flesh on our bones,' she has said.

Jamil comes from a South Asian family of modest means, and has spoken about the bullying, racism and sexual harassment she endured, as well as the negative self-image she developed from a steady diet of glossy women's magazines featuring weight-loss and beauty tips. She suffered from anorexia during her teens, but at seventeen, while recovering from a serious spinal injury suffered in a car accident, she realised that she had been conditioned to hate her body by a culture that profits from the self-loathing of young girls.

From her position within the entertainment industry, which feeds on the same insecurities that once plagued her and has too often fostered a hostile climate for women, Jamil is well-placed to encourage and lead on meaningful change. Through continuously alerting body-positivity issues and through her willingness to criticise her peers and the structure of the entertainment industry, Jamil is a positive and visible role model for millions across the globe.

Josephine Baker

Performer
3 June 1906 – 12 April 1975
United States of America and France

The world came to know of Josephine Baker's mesmerising talent in the 1920s, but she first stepped onstage at the age of one, accompanying her mother during a song-and-dance act. Her parents were struggling entertainers in St Louis, Missouri, and Freda Josephine McDonald was raised in poverty. At thirteen, she ran away from home, surviving on the little money she earned from busking on the streets, and married – briefly – at fifteen, taking her husband's surname, Baker. She joined a musical troupe, later moving to New York. There she lit up stages as a dancer and became one of the top-earning chorus girls in vaudeville.

Baker later travelled to Paris to work in an all-Black revue. She was an instant hit. Her stunning performances (one featuring her now-iconic banana skirt) saw her career flourish over the next decade in Europe, making her one of the highest-paid performers in the world.

Growing up in the US, Baker had often encountered aggressive racism, but in 1936 she decided to give her homeland another chance, performing on Broadway as one of the stars of *The Ziegfeld Follies*. Disillusioned by persistent hostility and threats, she returned to Paris, and became a French citizen. Racist American reviews had no impact on her stardom in Europe, and she continued to sing, dance and perform in films.

One of the brightest stars of the twentieth century, Baker was also highly respected for her humanitarian work and social justice advocacy. During World War II, she contributed to the Resistance as an ambulance driver, a Red Cross nurse, a spy (transmitting messages written with invisible ink on sheet music or hidden in her underwear) and, of course, as an entertainer for the troops. In 1963, she spoke during the Civil Rights March in Washington, DC, sharing her experiences of racial injustice in the US. An activist and icon loved by many, when Baker died in Paris in 1975, 20,000 mourners attended her funeral.

Junko Tabei

Mountaineer
22 September 1939 – 20 October 2016
Japan

Junko Tabei, a fragile girl prone to pneumonia, ascended her first mountain when she was ten. In 2016, terminally ill with cancer, she climbed Mount Fuji. In between, this petite woman achieved an enviable reputation as a barrier-breaking mountaineer.

Tabei reached the summit of Mount Everest in 1975 – the first woman to do so. (In fact, she was the first woman to climb *all* Seven Summits – the tallest mountains on each continent.) Eschewing the traditional roles expected of Japanese women, and ignoring the male-dominated clubs that did not admit female members, Tabei connected with other women interested in mountaineering and helped form the Ladies' Climbing Club in 1969.

Cutting her career as a teacher short, Tabei edited a science journal, tutored English and taught piano in order to fund her climbing ambitions. Although she was told frequently that it was inappropriate for women to seek such challenges, she secured sponsorship for the Everest expedition. Her husband, a respected mountaineer himself, supported her, caring for their children when she was away on expeditions.

The Everest climb was precarious. With 2,800 metres left to the summit, an avalanche buried the fifteen-member party. Sherpas came to the rescue, and there were no casualties – but Tabei and others were injured. Nevertheless, Tabei pushed herself upward. Later, it transpired that the Sherpas could not carry up enough oxygen for more than one climber. Alongside Sherpa Ang Tsering, the party nominated Tabei to continue to the summit and make history.

In 2000, Tabei obtained her postgraduate degree, writing on the environmental degradation of Everest as the result of overactivity. She became the director of the Himalayan Adventure Trust of Japan, dedicating the last years of her life to preserving the ecology of the great mountains, which had given it so much meaning.

Katherine Johnson

Mathematician
26 August 1918 – 24 February 2020
United States of America

When Creola Katherine Johnson was a girl, she counted everything: dishes in the cupboard, silverware, stairs. She worked out the number of steps between her family home in West Virginia, and their church. Decades later, Johnson calculated the trajectories of the first manned American spacecraft to orbit the Earth and land on the moon.

This is an extraordinary feat for anyone. It is all the more impressive considering Katherine Johnson was an African American woman, working as a mathematician during a time when racism and discrimination against both groups were normalised in the US, and it was comparatively difficult for African American women to receive a higher education. But Johnson was a mathematics prodigy, admitted to the second grade before she was six and to high school at ten, and a university graduate at eighteen. She attributed her abilities to her father, a minimally schooled farmer and handyman who was gifted mathematically and made special efforts to educate her.

Johnson worked as a teacher, before being invited, in 1940, to join a graduate programme at West Virginia University – one of the three black students, and the only Black woman; yet she left when she became pregnant with her first child.

In 1953, she learned that the agency that would become the National Aeronautics and Space Administration was accepting Black women as research mathematicians. Johnson became a 'computer' – the designation applied only to humans then, working with slide rules. Seconded to the Flight Research Division for aerodynamics calculations, she stood out at once for her command of geometry. She remained there until the end of her career in 1986, working on projects of increasing complexity: moon orbits, lunar landings, splashdown windows, space navigational charts, the Shuttle programme and Mars mission plans.

So impeccable was her reputation that, after electronic computers were introduced, John Glenn – the first American to orbit Earth – requested that machine calculations for his flight be checked by Johnson first.

In 2015, she was awarded the Presidential Medal of Freedom by Barack Obama.

Lea T

Fashion Model
Born 19 February 1982
Brazil and Italy

Throughout her childhood, Lea T felt 'different'. Born Leandro Medeiros Cerezo in Brazil and assigned male at birth, she would eventually become the first transgender model to represent a global beauty campaign. However, becoming this successful was never going to be easy for Lea T.

Lea T endured years of alienation from her Catholic family, and experienced bewilderment about her own gender, which she could not define. She would embrace her true nature only as an adult. Her friend Riccardo Tisci, then an aspiring fashion designer and later the creative director of Givenchy, supported and encouraged her. No longer denying her reality, Lea T began the process of gender reassignment. She felt lonely and ostracised, enduring stares, mockery, groping and menacing behaviour as she went about her daily business.

Lea T worked as Tisci's personal assistant, becoming his muse as he rose through the ranks at Givenchy. She eventually became a top model – and proudly transgender. Lea T rocked the fashion industry, was appointed the face of Redken and appeared in magazines from *Vanity Fair* to *Love*. French *Vogue* featured a stunning, controversial nude portrait of her. In Rio de Janeiro in 2016, Lea T became the first publicly transgender person to participate in an Olympic ceremony, leading the Brazilian team into the stadium on a bicycle.

'Society separates [people into groups],' Lea T has said, 'treating the oppressed in one way and the rest normally and even with a certain superiority ... It doesn't make sense. But it is up to those who are in the [oppressed] group to raise the flag, if they want to. I make a point of saying that I am trans ... It is important to use that visibility with pride. If I had not ... we would not have opened the doors.'

Lee Tai-young

Lawyer and Judge
Born 10 August 1914 – 16 December 1998
South Korea

Korea's National Judicial Examination (abolished in 2017) was notoriously difficult for lawyers. Candidates often studied hours a day, for years, to pass it. In 1952, Lee Tai-young became the first woman to pass it. Having experienced high-pressure environments as a law-school student – nursing her baby between classes – she moved to a rooming house for several months to cram for the exam, with the support of her husband and family. She later said: 'Females in Korea simply don't have the resources, time or encouragement to take a year off to study for one test.'

Tai-young not only observed the demands on women in ultra-patriarchal Korean society, but voiced her objections to those demands too, from an early age. As a child she gave presentations interrogating the preference for sons over daughters and the discouragement of girls' schooling. She decided to become a lawyer when she was seven years old. She faced many setbacks on her journey. When Seoul National University opened the faculty to women in 1946, she was finally able to enrol at law school. But under wartime occupation, Tai-young's husband was imprisoned for 'anti-Japanese' activity. To support their three children, she took in washing and sewing and sang on radio.

Once she had passed her exams and established herself as a lawyer, Tai-young opened the Women's Legal Counselling Centre in 1957, providing services to poor women. For decades, the Centre helped more than 10,000 women a year who needed representation and advice, mainly in cases concerning marriage, divorce, custody, schooling, property and domestic violence. She also helped drive changes to South Korea's judicial system, seeing the establishment of Seoul Family Court and revisions to laws that penalised women in civil cases. Tai-young and her husband took part in the 1976 Myeongdong Declaration calling for full democracy. She and other leaders were arrested by authorities and penalised severely. Nonetheless, she received many awards for her work, published fifteen books, and eventually transitioned from a lawyer to judge.

Leymah Gbowee

Peace Activist
Born 1 February 1972
Liberia

When the First Liberian Civil War broke out in 1989, seventeen-year-old Leymah Gbowee and her family fled, becoming refugees in Ghana. Later she returned to Liberia, trained as a trauma counsellor and worked with former child soldiers.

During the Second Liberian Civil War, Gbowee witnessed violence, rape, hunger, death and impoverishment. She joined the Women in Peacebuilding Network, and later formed an initiative called Women of Liberia Mass Action for Peace, which expanded to over 2,500 women from all faiths. They protested the war publicly and peacefully, and even vowed to withhold sex to force their men to speak up in favour of peace.

In 2003 the protestors, dressed in white, confronted President Charles Taylor. The President held the ultimate responsibility for the violence. He refused to see them, but the protestors stood their ground. He then agreed to see only ten of them, but Gbowee declined to compromise. He gave in.

In her address to the President, Gbowee didn't use a single aggressive word. She said: 'We are tired of war. We are tired of running. We are tired of begging ... We are tired of our children being raped.' Taylor declared that he would attend peace talks, but nothing came of this pledge.

Months later, led by Gbowee, 200 women protestors followed Taylor's representatives to talks in Ghana. They barricaded the negotiating warlords, refusing to leave unless a peace deal was signed. Guards threatened them, but they wouldn't budge. This act of resistance led to a peace agreement. Taylor went into exile and was eventually apprehended and sentenced to fifty years' imprisonment. Liberia hasn't been at war since.

A global voice for sustainable conflict resolution, Gbowee advocates for women as agents of peace. Her efforts paved the path for the first female president of Liberia, Ellen Johnson Sirleaf, with whom Gbowee shared the 2011 Nobel Peace Prize.

Linda Sarsour

Civil Rights Activist
Born 19 March 1980
United States of America

Linda Sarsour was a regular Brooklyn girl whose parents had emigrated from Palestine in the 1970s. She was Muslim, but not visibly: her name was atypical, and she didn't wear a headscarf until she was nineteen.

Sarsour married at seventeen and attended college, intending to become a schoolteacher. But in the aftermath of the 9/11 terrorist attacks, as American Muslims felt their civil rights come under threat, Sarsour encountered serious harassment and saw men in her community being rounded up. Incensed by the spectacle of innocent people facing violence and injustice, she began volunteering at the Arab American Association of New York (AAANY).

The organisation's founder, Basemah Atweh, became her mentor, but died tragically in a car crash in 2005. Sarsour became AAANY's executive director, leading campaigns against discriminatory immigration policy, mass incarceration, Islamophobia and invasive police tactics, as well as promoting voter registration and changing attitudes in her community. Blunt, dynamic, debate-ready and easily traversing different age, ethnic and religious groups, Sarsour became a force in New York politics, able to reach older, conservative Muslims and build bridges with activists in other communities.

Sansour became involved in the Black Lives Matter (BLM) movement after the 2014 police shooting that galvanised it, and has worked in-depth with BLM since then. A regular commentator in American news media, in 2017 she was named one of *TIME*'s 100 Most Influential People. In the same year she was recruited to co-chair the Women's March on Washington, held on the day of President Donald Trump's inauguration.

Sarsour has faced intense hatred and death threats because of her activism and defiant stance. She is often accused of being Islamist and anti-Jewish by right-wing critics, but has amply demonstrated her support for civil over religious law, and her indefatigable support for victims of all forms of racist violence.

Loujain al-Hathloul

Women's Rights Activist
Born 31 July 1989
Saudi Arabia

In 2014, Saudi citizen Loujain al-Hathloul was arrested upon returning from the United Arab Emirates at the wheel of a car and jailed for seventy-three days. However, the young woman had *deliberately* set out to challenge Saudi Arabia's proscription against female drivers, live-streaming her trip as part of a 'Women to Drive' campaign.

Al-Hathloul's mother had raised her daughters never to be afraid of speaking out, and her father and brother had taught her to drive, defying the ban. When she moved to Canada for university, she drove everywhere she could, exulting in this relative luxury. Al-Hathloul continued to challenge her country's suffocating restrictions on women's independence. She has also protested the 'male guardianship' laws that forbid women to make major decisions without a man's approval. Her influence in Saudi Arabia grew as she campaigned peacefully for women's freedom – at considerable personal risk.

In 2018, after attending an UN-sponsored meeting in Geneva to speak on Saudi women's lack of rights, al-Hathloul was seized by Emirati security forces in the UAE and deported to Saudi Arabia, then arrested along with ten other women activists. Seven were let go; she remained incarcerated.

Shortly after her arrest, the driving ban for women in Saudi Arabia was lifted. When al-Hathloul's family visited her, she would ask how women outside were enjoying their new prerogative, keeping disclosures about her own situation to a minimum. Yet she was enduring torture in prison, including electrocution and threats of dismemberment and rape.

In late 2020 al-Hathloul, visibly weakened from, among other things, a hunger strike she staged in protest against being denied contact with her family, appeared at the start of her trial in a special 'terrorism court'. She was sentenced to five years and eight months in prison in December 2020. Saudi authorities fear her prominence as an activist and know that al-Hathloul enjoys considerable international support. She has since been released on strict probation conditions and faces a five-year travel ban. Despite her release from prison, Loujain is far from free.

Mae C Jemison

Doctor and Astronaut
Born 17 October 1956
United States of America

Growing up in Chicago, Mae Jemison was full of ambitions: she dreamed of becoming a fashion designer, an archaeologist, a dancer, an astronaut... Her curiosity was endless, and so were the possibilities.

But young Mae was inspired most by Nichelle Nichols, the African American actress who famously portrayed Lieutenant Uhura in the *Star Trek* television series. Seeing a starship officer who looked like her kept her closely connected to the idea of taking flight into space.

Jemison was a brilliant student and graduated from high school with honours. She obtained a scholarship to study at Stanford University, and pursued degrees in both Chemical Engineering and African American Studies. After graduating, she decided to study medicine at Cornell University as well and became a doctor. She then travelled in that capacity, practising at a Cambodian refugee camp in Thailand; at twenty-seven, she became the regional Peace Corps medical officer for Sierra Leone and Liberia, in which role she continued for two and a half years.

In 1986, Jemison pursued her dream of becoming an astronaut, and, accordingly, applied to the National Aeronautics and Space Administration. She wasn't selected but she tried again the following year – and was chosen from among 2,000 applicants.

After an intense year of training, Jemison made history by becoming the first Black woman in space. During her mission, she conducted various experiments on bone cells, weightlessness and motion sickness, using herself and the crew as research subjects.

But Jemison didn't stop only at travelling to the stars herself. After leaving NASA, she started a foundation that would go on to lead the joint NASA/Defense Department 100 Year Starship project, which fosters developments that will aid human interstellar spaceflight within a hundred years.

'We have to have a vision that works across generations,' Jemison has said.

Malala Yousafzai

Activist and Author
Born 12 July 1997
Pakistan

Born and raised in Pakistan's Swat Valley, Malala is the daughter of an educational activist and has always been devoted to learning. When she was a pre-teen, Pakistani Taliban militants banned girls' education in her region and blew up more than 100 girls' schools. Malala rejected this unlawful edict, involving herself in social activism at the age of just twelve.

Malala wrote a pseudonymous BBC Urdu blog that detailed her life under the Pakistani Taliban occupation. This led to a *New York Times* documentary about her life, and she was subsequently nominated for the International Children's Peace Prize by Desmond Tutu. Malala became well-known nationally and internationally for her advocacy of children's and educational issues. Then, in 2012, after seeing Malala on the news, the Taliban targeted her directly. As she and her school mates boarded the bus one day, an extremist followed them asking: 'Which of you is Malala?' Upon being identified, the gunman shot her in the head.

Malala was rushed to the hospital, while news of the attack generated a storm around the globe. Support for Malala came from every corner, including offers of medical assistance. After receiving treatment in Pakistan, she was flown to the UK for further surgery.

During her recovery, she continued to think of ways to help girls in the Swat Valley. Malala met with world leaders and focused international attention on the issues that had resulted in her shooting. Everyone praised her courage and passion. In 2013, during a speech at the UN, she said: 'They thought that the bullet would silence us, but they failed.'

Today, the Malala Fund, a non-profit organisation bearing Yousafzai's name, drives solutions to remove barriers to girls' education, as Malala has continued fighting for girls' education throughout the world, while also pursuing her own. After attending Edgbaston High School in the UK, she completed a degree at Oxford University in Philosophy, Politics and Economics. In 2014, she was awarded the Nobel Peace Prize, becoming the youngest-ever Nobel Laureate.

Margaret Busby

Publisher and Writer
Born 11 October 1944
Ghana and the United Kingdom

Despite slow progress, increasing numbers of British writers of colour are finding themselves on high-street bookshelves and literary-prize shortlists. Far fewer occupy senior publishing positions, but that will change, too. The inevitable, however, once seemed inconceivable – and times would have changed much more slowly without Margaret Busby.

Born in Ghana and educated in England, Busby frequently sought out books by writers from diverse backgrounds, absent from school curricula. When she met fellow undergraduate Clive Allison at a party in London, they discovered their shared aspirations to publish affordable books, and formed Allison & Busby in 1967.

Lacking distribution, they sold poetry paperbacks to passers-by in the street, even knocking on car windows. Busby took on other work to keep afloat, sustained by her desire to publish books she believed in. She was often underestimated: Allison, a white man, was assumed to be the head of the company, and Busby, his employee.

When Busby came across a much-rejected novel by a young African American writer, Sam Greenlee, she took a different view. *The Spook Who Sat by the Door* became Allison & Busby's first prose title and a major success, translated into multiple languages and adapted for the screen.

Busby disdained the competitive atmosphere forced on Black writers and writers of colour because there were so few opportunities for them to be published. She wanted authors to be able to create freely, without such pressures – and went on to publish many illustrious writers such as Chester Himes, CLR James and Nuruddin Farah.

In 1992 Busby was commissioned to compile a seminal anthology, *Daughters of Africa*, featuring the writing of more than 200 women of African descent in over 1,000 pages. Her sequel was published in 2019 – a reminder that much still needs to change, and that the right woman for the job is still on the case. The money generated by the book will pay for a MA bursary – the Margaret Busby New Daughters of Africa award – at SOAS University of London, for a female African student.

Maria da Penha

Women's Rights Activist
Born 1 February 1945
Brazil

In 1976, biopharmacist Maria da Penha married her Colombian fiancé, economist Marcos Antonio Viveros. They had three daughters. Then, suddenly, the violence began.

After Vivero was granted Brazilian citizenship, he began abusing his wife and children, striking them, tying them up and forcing the girls into cold showers as 'punishment'. Da Penha made no official complaint: at the time, domestic violence was not a special category in the eyes of the law. 'We weren't even aware of this expression,' da Penha has said. 'You just had a "bad husband".'

In 1983, as da Penha slept, Viveros shot her. She was rushed to the hospital by neighbours. The bullet lodged in her spine, and she became a paraplegic. Viveros claimed he had been fending off burglars, which the police accepted as truth. When da Penha was released from hospital, paralysed, Viveros isolated her from friends and family. She made covert preparations to escape – but one day, Viveros tried to electrocute her as she bathed.

Fortunately, da Penha survived, and left Viveros. For the next nineteen years, she fought to see him jailed; he was tried twice and found guilty, but went free each time on appeal. In 2002, Viveros was sentenced to eight years' imprisonment, but was released in 2003.

Meanwhile, da Penha had campaigned for changes in the law, even taking her case to the Organisation of American States. In 2006, the 'Maria da Penha Law' was passed: Brazil now recognises multiple forms of violence against women and sets stricter punishments for abusers – a change that has had a life-saving impact on countless women.

Da Penha has not ceased campaigning. In 2009, she founded the Instituto Maria da Penha, a non-profit organisation to raise women's awareness of their rights and strengthen the Maria da Penha Law through education and training.

Maria Walanda Maramis

Activist
1 December 1872 – 22 April 1924
Indonesia

In 1969, the government of Indonesia declared Walanda a National Hero for her work toward the emancipation of women.

Born Maria Josephine Catherine Maramis, aged six Maramis and her two siblings became orphans following their parents' deaths from disease. Born and raised on Sulawesi, the fourth-largest island in what was then the Dutch East Indies, the children were adopted by their uncle. According to custom, whereby girls were primed for marriage from an early age, Maramis and her sister were educated only to basic level. They were taught to read and write, and received some science and history tuition. (Accordingly, Dutch colonial authorities proscribed higher education for Indigenous women.)

Maramis did marry, and her name changed to Maria Walanda Maramis. She then began writing an opinion column for a local newspaper. Her topics were motherhood, and women's role in caring for the health, well-being and education of their families. Then, in 1917, she founded PIKAT. PIKAT is an Indonesian acronym for 'A Mother's Love for Her Children'. The organisation taught women skills such as cooking, sewing and childcare. PIKAT spread to other, far-flung islands in the archipelago. In 1918, a PIKAT school opened on Sulawesi, funded by a loan Walanda secured from a Dutch trader.

PIKAT offered women a network through which they could exchange skills and information. Driven by her wish to empower women, Walanda taught them to build their knowledge base in ways that would serve them directly, in the absence of formal education. Walanda sent her own two daughters to teacher training school in Batavia (now Jakarta), and they went on to teach professionally – one maintaining a role with PIKAT. Walanda also worked for political change, arguing for women's right to vote for their local representatives. In 1921 this right was granted.

Marjane Satrapi

Comics Artist, Writer and Film Director
Born 22 November 1969
Iran and France

Marjane Satrapi is one of those artists whose restless urge to create knows no bounds. She is best known as a comics artist, particularly for her autobiographical masterpieces *Persepolis* and *Persepolis 2*. She also co-directed the film adaptation of *Persepolis*, and has written and directed other films, including the Marie Curie biopic *Radioactive* (2019).

Satrapi grew up in Tehran, in a Marxist family that had to tread carefully after the 1979 Islamic Revolution (her beloved uncle was executed; she was his last visitor). An intelligent, outspoken teenager, Satrapi read ceaselessly, listened to punk music and took risks with the strict modesty laws. Her parents, worried that she was courting arrest by the morality police, sent her away to Austria aged fourteen for her own safety – a decision all the more understandable after their neighbours' house was bombed, and Satrapi's friend killed.

In Vienna, Satrapi attended a *lyceé*. After suffering a period of alienation, finding herself forced to change residences and also experiencing a failed relationship, Satrapi was in difficulties. She became homeless for some months and nearly died from bronchitis. On her return to Iran, she became depressed and suicidal. Satrapi then reached a turning point, and decided instead to live ferociously. She studied art, married briefly, then left Iran for France in 1993.

In 1995, receiving Art Spiegelman's seminal comic *Maus* as a gift, she experienced an epiphany. Recognising the power of the medium, she began to work on what would become *Persepolis* in 1999. Her book was an international success and was translated into twenty-four languages. Through witty writing, and spare visuals with an expressionist edge, Satrapi simultaneously depicts the unpleasant aspects of life in post-revolutionary Iran and defuses Western ignorance about the lives of Iranians. The story is nuanced, universal, poignant and honest.

Satrapi continues to create comics and work in film. Although her spirit remains restless, she is grounded in her art.

Mary Golda Ross

Engineer
9 August 1908 – 29 April 2008
United States of America

Mary Golda Ross could claim several 'firsts' and 'onlys' in her long life. She was often the only girl in her maths, chemistry and physics classes; she was the first female Native American engineer; the first woman to work in engineering at the aerospace giant Lockheed Corporation and she was among the first engineers at Lockheed's super-secretive 'Skunk Works' aeronautics base. She was also the only woman on the programme.

Ross's great-great-grandfather was the Cherokee Nation chief John Ross, who led thousands of his people to Talequah during their tragic forced migration by the US government in the 1830s. Mary was herself born in Tahlequah, Oklahoma, capital of the Cherokee Nation, and raised by her grandparents. She was a keen learner. After obtaining her BA, she worked as a teacher for some years before earning her MA in Mathematics from Colorado State College of Education in 1938.

During World War Two, Ross was hired by the Lockheed Corporation. She worked on key engineering issues for the P-38 Lightning, then the world's fastest airplane and a critical success in the war. Impressed, Lockheed dispatched her to the University of California to pursue an aeronautics engineering certification. Later, Ross joined the founding forty members of the top-secret (and still-extant) Advanced Development Programs (known as 'Skunk Works') team, responsible for many aviation and aerospace innovations.

Over Ross's successful career, her research contributed to design concepts for space travel – her first love. She co-authored the third volume of NASA's *Planetary Flight Handbook*, which covers travel to Mars and Venus. She also worked on the Agena Rocket's orbital dynamics. After her retirement in 1973, Ross worked as a mentor, encouraging young women and Native Americans to enter the sciences. A long-time member of the Society of Women Engineers, she also supported the American Indians in Science and Engineering Society and the Council of Energy Resource Tribes.

Mary Jane Seacole

Nurse and Entrepreneur
23 November 1805 – 14 May 1881
Jamaica and the United Kingdom

Mary Grant, an unlikely hero of the Crimean War, was born in Jamaica. Her father was a Scottish lieutenant, and her mother was a Jamaican 'doctress', or traditional healer, who ran a renowned Kingston boarding house in which many British garrison personnel convalesced from serious illnesses.

Mary married an Englishman named Seacole in 1836. Together they set up a shop, but sadly he died prematurely, shortly followed by her mother. Mary rebuilt the boarding house her mother had run, which had been destroyed by fire, and turned a profit. Then she travelled to Panama, where she ran a hotel and continued developing as a reputable doctress herself.

In 1854, Seacole resolved to tend to her military 'sons' fighting in Crimea, hoping to join Florence Nightingale's nursing corps. She arrived in London with references, but was rejected by government recruiters (on account of racism, she believed). Nevertheless, she found a business partner and set off for the Crimea, building 'The British Hotel' near Balaklava, behind the lines, from salvaged materials. A *de facto* field hospital and rest home for wounded soldiers, it became famous, and prospered. But Seacole also ventured onto the battlefield numerous times, selflessly bringing aid to soldiers there and nursing them, at great risk.

When the war ended, Seacole went back to Britain with almost no money. Her financial woes were reported in the press, and a fund was established to aid her. Many prominent figures and veterans showed their respect by contributing, and a three-day festival was held in her honour in Royal Surrey Gardens in 1857, attended by 80,000 people (although she saw few of the proceeds).

Seacole published a well-received memoir, and saw out her life in decent straits, although she was neglected by history. Her London grave was rediscovered and restored in 1973 and in 2004, she was voted Greatest Black Briton. In 2016, her statue was erected at St Thomas' Hospital, Southbank. In such small ways, she has re-entered the popular consciousness, as is her due.

Mary Kom

Boxer
Born 1 March 1983
India

Mary Kom – born Mangte Chungneijang – was raised in a village in Manipur, India, by her parents who were both poor tenant farmers. She looked after her younger siblings and helped with chores, but she was determined to do more to ease her family's circumstances.

Kom was always athletic. At school, she played football and volleyball and ran track. She decided to pursue her talents further, and at fifteen, she went to study at the sports academy in Imphal, the state capital. Her coach noticed that Kom wasn't very tall and didn't appear strong; even her tracksuit was torn. But he also noticed her willpower, grit and single-mindedness.

In 2000, Kom decided to take up boxing. She didn't tell her family, but one day her father heard a rumour that a girl from their tribe was boxing. He later saw Kom's photograph in the newspaper. When her mother approached Kom to enquire further, she found her daughter with a newly won medal. Despite her success and obvious talent, Kom's parents disapproved. They did not want her to risk a physical injury or ruin her chances of marrying. This didn't happen, and Kom met a man named Karung Onkholer, married him, and they had twin sons. Kom then took a break to focus on their family. She was hesitant to return to boxing, but her husband was her biggest supporter. He even quit his own work to care for their sons, so that Kom could continue with hers.

Kom has won the gold medal six times at the AIBA World Boxing Championships: a world record. Altogether, 'Magnificent Mary' (as she is known) is also the only boxer, male or female, to have won eight of the competition's medals. She was the only Indian female boxer selected for the 2012 London Summer Olympics, where she took bronze. Since then, she has opened a boxing academy in Imphal, and was nominated to serve in India's Parliament. 'Take me as an example and don't give up,' Magnificent Mary has said.

Maya Angelou

Writer and Civil Rights Activist
4 April 1928 – 28 May 2014
United States of America

St Louis-born Marguerite Annie Johnson would become famous as 'Maya', the nickname her brother, Bailey, Jr, gave her. After their parents' divorce, Maya and Bailey, Jr moved to Arkansas to live with their grandmother, with whom Angelou shared a special bond.

After a few short years with their grandmother, the children moved in with their mother, who now lived with a man named Freeman. When Angelou was only seven, Freeman raped her. She didn't tell anyone for a while, but shortly after the truth came out, Freeman was found dead. The event traumatised young Maya, who now believed her words were capable of killing people. It triggered mutism: she didn't speak for five years.

Angelou and her brother moved back with their grandmother. During this time, she read copiously. One day, a woman Angelou's grandmother called 'Sister Flowers' walked into the shop and invited the girl to tea. 'Your grandmother says you read a lot,' she said. 'Every chance you get. That's good, but not good enough.' She introduced Angelou to poetry, and the importance of the spoken word. Slowly, she helped Angelou overcome her trauma.

As an adult, Angelou worked as a San Francisco cable car driver, sex worker, actress, newspaper foreign correspondent and editor, modern dancer and – significantly – an influential coordinator in the Civil Rights Movement, collaborating with Malcolm X and Martin Luther King, Jr. Her book *I Know Why the Caged Bird Sings* (the first of seven works that expanded and innovated the autobiographical form) launched her literary career. She would write poetry, plays, essays and screenplays as well, and recited her poem 'On the Pulse of Morning' at Bill Clinton's first inauguration as US President.

Writer, performer, activist, mother: Angelou began in silence, but left a legacy of words that will endure for generations to come.

Maya Lin

Architect and Artist
Born 5 October 1959
United States of America

Maya Lin's parents emigrated from China to the US, and she was born and raised in Athens, Ohio. She was a happy child there, fond of reading, building model towns and birdwatching. Nature inspired her constantly.

Lin attended Yale University to study Field Zoology – but changed her mind and chose to pursue a degree in Architecture instead. In 1980, during her final year, she saw a poster for a competition inviting design submissions for a Vietnam War Veterans Memorial in Washington, DC. Lin decided to make this her last project as a student, and submitted her plans to the competition. There were over 1,400 entries, but her design stood out – and won. At just twenty-one years old, she became the first woman to design a memorial on the National Mall.

Many people were unhappy with the minimalism of Lin's charismatic design; others didn't approve of her arrangement of the names of nearly 58,000 servicemen in chronological order. Yet her vision became a reality in 1982 and the memorial has since become a much-loved site with around 3 million visitors every year. The design is often described as being ahead of its time.

The memorial is not the only demonstration of how Lin looks to the future. A true environmentalist, she tries to use recycled materials in her work. Global warming, endangered species and loss of biodiversity all concern her. 'If I could do something to help us stop degrading the planet,' she has said, 'if I could help in any way – that's what I'm striving to do.' In works such as *Disappearing Bodies of Water*, in which Lin examines what is left of areas such as the Red Sea, the Arctic ice shelf and Lake Chad, she focuses on environmental threats and spreads awareness about what is happening in the natural world.

Lin had always wanted to make a difference. As a memorialist, an environmentalist and an artist of distinction, she has done just that.

Mazlan Othman

Astrophysicist
Born 11 December 1951
Malaysia

As a girl in Seremban, Malaysia, Mazlan Othman wanted to study English literature or arts. Her exceptional talent in mathematics became apparent at school, however, and she fell in love with physics at thirteen. Her family had encouraged her to become a doctor, and she did choose science, after all – but medicine wasn't the field she wanted to explore.

Othman went on to receive a university scholarship to study in New Zealand, where she discovered astrophysics. She felt this discipline offered her everything: philosophy, aesthetics, scientific possibility ... and mystery. In 1981, she received her PhD and became her country's first astrophysicist.

Countries such as the US, Russia and China, with prominent space agencies and advanced research capabilities, led the field of space exploration; but Othman wanted Malaysia to contribute. She returned there after completing her education, determined to attract more Malaysians to the study of the cosmos, and spent nearly a decade developing university courses in astrophysics and spreading public awareness about space issues. In 1990, she was appointed by the prime minister to lead the development of the national planetarium in Kuala Lumpur.

Othman has worked tirelessly to lay a foundation for her chosen branch of science in her country and represents Malaysia at conventions all over the world. She was appointed Director of the United Nations Office for Outer Space Affairs in Vienna in 1999 and again in 2007 and was also the founding Director of the Malaysian National Space Agency, where her pioneering work saw the first Malaysian astronaut in space.

As a female scientist in the male-dominated field of astrophysics, Othman believes that her unyielding passion has played the biggest role in her success, keeping her focused only on putting her country on the map for space exploration.

Mercedes Sosa

Singer
9 July 1935 – 4 October 2009
Argentina

In the late 1960s, the population of Latin America comprised approximately 286 million people – and Mercedes Sosa was their voice. In a career that extended over six decades, seventy albums and multiple Latin Grammy Awards, Sosa went on to gain a truly global presence.

Sosa was born into a family with French, Spanish and Indigenous heritage in northwest Argentina. She became a professional singer after winning a radio competition aged just fifteen. Soon, Sosa was recognised as a pioneer of nueva canción music, the counterpart to the US folk music scene, with impassioned songs describing the political upheavals then underway and the struggles of ordinary people.

Sosa was an international star by 1976, the year Argentina's military launched a coup and established a right-wing dictatorship, during whose control over 30,000 people would be 'disappeared'. She initially refused to leave Argentina, although her outspoken leftist convictions made her a target. After her arrest in 1979 during a concert (along with everyone in the audience), and her release thanks to pressure from around the world, she went into exile in Paris and Madrid. By 1982 the military junta, weakened by the Falklands War, were becoming less powerful in Argentina and Sosa was able to return to her country. She gave a series of legendary, triumphant concerts in Buenos Aires. In later years, she would be able to tour widely, performing in venues including Carnegie Hall in New York and the Sistine Chapel and the Colosseum in Rome.

'La Negra', as Sosa was known because of her dark hair and Amerindian heritage, sang songs of resistance with great emotional resonance, in a powerful, earthy voice. She earned the devotion of millions with hits such as 'Gracias a la Vida' (Thanks to Life), which is considered her signature song.

Sosa's music reflected the lives of people across South America, and the world. 'I didn't choose to sing for people,' she said shortly before her death. 'Life chose me.'

Michaela Coel

Writer, Producer and Actor
Born 1 October 1987
United Kingdom

Even in an era of ground-breaking television, Michaela Coel stands out. She has written and performed professionally since 2006 but her big screen breaks came in 2015 and 2020 with sitcom *Chewing Gum* and dramatic series *I May Destroy You*, both widely acclaimed.

Born in London to Ghanaian immigrants, Coel and her sister were raised by their mother on a council estate where there very few Black families, and regularly endured racial slurs and vandalism. Intense, curious and restless, Coel participated in youth theatre and, at twenty-two, enrolled in the Guildhall School of Music and Drama – the first Black woman admitted there in years.

At Guildhall, Coel wrote a darkly humorous one-woman show. A production company approached her to transform it into the series *Chewing Gum*, centring on a young woman ready to lose her virginity. Coel had never written for television before and was frustrated by the industry's culture of excluding creatives at certain stages of production. Thankfully, she was involved in almost every creative aspect of the show, which subsequently became a huge hit. She won two British Academy of Film and Television Arts (BAFTA) awards in 2016, for comedy performance and for writing.

Giving the distinguished MacTaggart Lecture at the Edinburgh International Television Festival in 2018, Coel shocked the audience by citing, thoughtfully and intelligently, her experience of racism in the television industry – and of being sexually assaulted. She used that painful incident as the basis of *I May Destroy You*. Again, Coel showed her integrity as an artist, turning down a $1 million offer from Netflix so that she could retain full rights and creative control of the show, which aired on the BBC instead. The series, which is experimental and pushes many boundaries, earned much critical praise, and won two BAFTA television awards.

The self-aware 'misfit' Coel is now a show business insider, contributing to positive change in the industry while creating some of the most original programming in years.

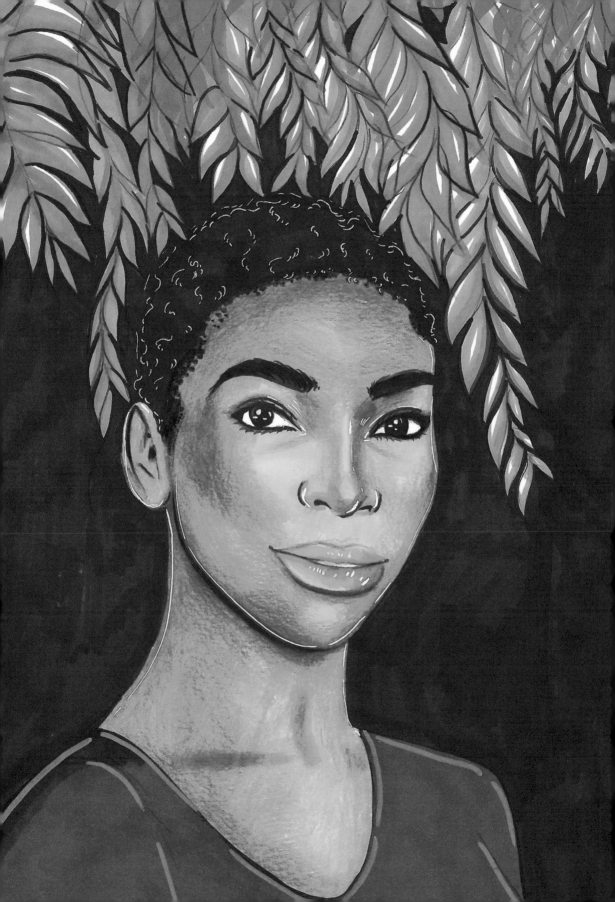

Michelle Obama

Lawyer, Writer and Former First Lady
Born 17 January 1964
United States of America

Michelle Obama is a lawyer, writer and became the first African American First Lady when her husband, Barack Obama, became President of the United States in 2009. As First Lady, Obama focused her attention on social issues, including education. Her own parents had not attended college, but always emphasised the importance of studying hard. She was a brilliant student, and a National Honor Society graduate. Yet when she declared her interest in attending the prestigious Princeton University, her high school college counsellor tried to put her off applying, saying: 'I'm not sure you're Princeton material.' Michelle applied anyway – with success.

At Princeton, Obama became an assistant at the support centre for students of colour. She had quickly observed that the students at Princeton were majority-white and male. Her roommates were two white girls; the mother of one disapproved of her daughter sharing with a Black student and attempted to have her moved. Despite these prejudices, Obama completed her studies and attended law school at Harvard, before returning to her hometown, Chicago, in 1988. Working at a law firm there, she was assigned to mentor a summer associate named Barack, who asked her out; she declined at first, but eventually accepted. They married in 1992.

Michelle Obama had worked hard to become a lawyer, but decided that the law was not her true calling. She wanted to serve people directly, so she quit her corporate job and joined various community organisations, where she continued her work alongside the demands on her as a mother of two young girls.

Michelle Obama was a crucial part of her husband's campaign for presidential election. Her heartfelt speeches moved women and men alike. As First Lady, she campaigned relentlessly for women's empowerment, action against child obesity, the provision of better services for veterans and their families, equality for all, and for education for girls. Obama broke through the racial and gender divide and made her way into the hearts of the American people, inspiring millions across the world.

Mindy Kaling

Comedian, Producer and Writer
Born 22 June 1979
United States of America

Growing up, Mindy Kaling never saw anyone who looked like her on television, especially in comedy – but she still knew that what she wanted to do in life was to entertain people. She would sit in her mother's office after school and write comedy sketches, and every time her mother laughed, it made Kaling more determined that comedy could be her future.

At Dartmouth University, studying playwriting, Kaling fully immersed herself in the opportunities available, joining student performance groups and became a cartoonist for the university newspaper. After graduation, Kaling and her best friend Brenda Withers wrote a play titled *Matt & Ben*, which became so popular in New York that a TV network bought the television rights. They wanted to turn it into *Mindy & Brenda*, a story of two friends living in Brooklyn. The network informed Mindy and Brenda that they would have to audition for the roles of Mindy and Brenda, although they had written the parts based on their own lives. They did not get cast, and more 'conventionally attractive' actors got the parts instead. Sadly, actors of Indian origin were a rare sight in the US television industry, and mostly cast in stereotypical roles.

Fortunately, many other fantastic opportunities were to come. Kaling was hired as the first female staff writer for the US remake of the British hit comedy *The Office*, and was also a cast member for eight seasons, winning hearts as chatterbox Kelly Kapoor. Shortly afterwards, she created her own comedy show, *The Mindy Project*, which ran for six seasons. Kaling has also worked on movies by notable comedy directors, as a voice actor for animated films, produced films and authored *New York Times* bestsellers.

With Netflix, she has created and produced *Never Have I Ever*, an acclaimed coming-of-age series with an Indian-American girl at its centre, and a diverse cast – further paving the way for many other supposedly 'unconventional' talents.

The Mirabal Sisters

Revolutionaries
1924, 1925, 1935 – 25 November 1960
Dominican Republic

From 1930–61, the Dominican Republic was under the tyrannical rule of Rafael Trujillo. He spied on citizens, raped women, killed thousands of his own people and controlled the media. He also massacred over 15,000 Haitian migrants. The country was ruled through terror.

When Trujillo invited Minerva Mirabal and her family to a party and made sexual advances towards her there, she refused. He became her enemy, and imprisoned the sisters' father, who died shortly after his release. Minerva had studied law, but Trujillo prevented her from obtaining a law license. She joined an underground revolutionary group dedicated to ending the Trujillo regime. Her sisters María Teresa and Patria followed, as did all their husbands, all committing their lives to freedom and progress. When Trujillo became aware of their activities, he arrested the sisters and their husbands. After several months of international pressure, he let the women go, but their husbands remained imprisoned.

Trujillo considered the Mirabal sisters a threat and ordered their assassination. A trap was set. The sisters' husbands were transferred to a prison in a remote area. When the sisters were returning from a trip to see them one day, Trujillo's secret police intercepted them, beat them to death, placed their bodies in a car, and pushed it off a cliff. The truth behind the assassination was an open secret, and many historians believe it marked the limits of domestic and international tolerance of the Trujillo regime: six months later, in May 1961, a group of conspirators killed the dictator.

The fourth Mirabal sister, Dedé, had not joined the resistance, but played a pivotal role in sharing her sisters' stories, establishing a foundation and turning their home into a museum in their memory. The Dominican people call the Mirabal sisters, who are today revered as national heroes, 'las Mariposas' (the Butterflies).

Miriam Makeba

Singer
4 March 1932 – 9 November 2008
South Africa

Miriam Makeba was destined for greatness; her voice would mesmerise millions, not only in South Africa, but all over the world. However, she spent the first six months of her life in jail, after her mother – who was a *sangoma*, or traditional healer – was arrested for illegally brewing beer to sell, when Miriam was eighteen days old.

This was not the only difficulty Makeba would have to face during her life. She was also diagnosed with cancer, endured an abusive relationship, and was forced into exile while she was in her twenties. Through it all, singing would enable her to persevere.

Makeba was born in Johannesburg, the youngest of six siblings. Growing up, she sang in church, and at weddings and celebrations; people loved her voice. At seventeen, she married and became a mother to her only child. Her husband was violent towards her, and the relationship broke down. A while later, Makeba joined a group called The Cuban Brothers. They recorded their first hit in 1953, gaining national attention.

Along with her music career, Makeba also acted in an anti-apartheid docufiction film, *Come Back Africa* (1959), which earned her international recognition. She was very busy, travelling to London and the US to perform in prestigious jazz clubs, where she became a sensation. Makeba received much media coverage, met the biggest stars of the day and earned the sobriquet 'Mama Africa'.

Then, in 1960, the South African government cancelled her passport, and she went into a thirty-one-year exile in the US where she continued to record hit after hit and criticise South African apartheid. Having witnessed so much racial injustice in her old homeland, she could speak eloquently to those in her new one, and she contributed to the Civil Rights Movement in the US as well.

Alongside many other accolades, she became the first African woman to win a Grammy Award.

'Retire?' she once remarked. 'I will sing till the day I die.' And she did.

Misty Copeland

Ballerina
Born 10 September 1982
United States of America

A shy, introverted child, Misty Copeland never felt like she fitted in. Born in Kansas City, Missouri, she and her siblings moved with their mother and stepfather to Los Angeles. When their mother divorced, they lived in a motel, enduring constant financial struggles.

At thirteen, Copeland joined a ballet class at the San Pedro Boys and Girls Club. She felt an instant connection with the art: finally, she *belonged*. Thirteen is considered a late age to begin ballet training, but, inspired by ballerinas before her such as Raven Wilkinson and Paloma Herrera, Copeland picked it up quickly. She was deemed a prodigy.

Copeland travelled across the city every day to take classes, which was difficult, as her mother worked long hours and had little support. Her mother told Copeland she would have to quit; but thankfully Copeland's teacher, Cindy Bradley, was able to help. She offered to have Copeland to stay during the week as though she was a member of her own family, so that she could continue her training.

Within four years, Copeland was accepted by the American Ballet Theatre (ABT): a dream held by many in ballet but achieved by few – and even fewer people of colour. By 2007, Copeland was a soloist at ABT – only the second African American ballerina to attain such heights. In 2012, she assumed the lead in Stravinsky's *The Firebird*, to much acclaim; but after the New York premiere, Copeland withdrew with a severely fractured tibia bone in her leg. Doctors informed her that it was a career-ending injury. Yet Copeland persevered, and during her recovery, trained in whatever capacity she could. She put on her pointe shoes, dusted herself off and made her way back to the stage, front and centre.

In 2015, after performing in numerous starring roles, Copeland became the principal dancer at the ABT: the pinnacle of success in classical ballet. She is also the company's first African American principal dancer.

Na Hye-sok

Artist and Writer
28 April 1896 – 10 December 1948
Korea

Na Hye-sok was born in Japanese-occupied Korea, to a wealthy family that allowed her the freedom and resources to pursue higher education – a privilege many Korean girls didn't have. Korean tradition held that women's education was unnecessary: becoming a wife and mother was considered a woman's goal in life.

Hye-sok left Korea for Japan, in order to study at Tokyo Women's College of Arts, where she earned her BA in Western oil painting. Her family pressured her to marry, but she refused. Her aspirations were to write and paint. In 1918, she wrote her most famous work, a short story titled 'Kyonghui', which is among the earliest works of modern fiction by a Korean woman. It was also Korea's first published feminist story. Hye-sok's writing throughout her career has concerned with taboo subjects and women's roles and rights in society.

Under Japanese rule, Koreans lacked political representation, and Korean language and culture were disappearing fast. In 1919, the Korean independence movement began; Koreans protested peacefully, but were attacked by Japanese colonial authorities. Some were killed, and many jailed. Hye-sok was imprisoned for months. After her release, she joined forces with four other women and started a magazine, *Sinyoja* (*New Woman*), to bring women's voices and concerns into the media. Although the magazine was shut down after four issues, Hye-sok was already gaining recognition for her resistance against patriarchal traditions as well as for her beautiful paintings, which were acclaimed and exhibited nationally and internationally.

Hye-sok eventually married in 1920 and went with her husband on a three-year European tour. She continued to write and paint and became a mother of four. Unfortunately, her marriage ended in divorce. By Korean law, she lost her children and her property. She was shamed and shunned by society; even her family renounced her. Hye-sok died destitute and alone in a charity hospital, and the location of her grave is unknown.

Nadia Murad

Genocide Survivor and Activist
Born 1993
Iraq

One of eleven children raised by a single mother in a Yazidi village in northern Iraq, Nadia Murad once dreamed of owning a beauty salon. In August 2014, the village was occupied by ISIS, as part of the extremist force's invasion of the Yazidi region of Sinjar. Their goal was to eradicate the Yazidis through terrorism and violence; for Nadia, the worst was yet to come.

ISIS separated the men from the women and children. They shot 600 men, including six of Murad's brothers, and took the boys off to training camps. They gathered the older women, including Murad's mother, and killed them. Next, they took the young women to the ISIS-occupied city of Mosul, which held thousands of captive Yazidi girls. From there, Murad learned, they were to be sold as sex slaves.

Murad was sold several times over and suffered sexual violence by multiple men. She tried to escape, but the first time, she was caught, beaten and gang-raped. She attempted escape a second time, successfully, reaching an Arab home hours later. The family residing there hid her and smuggled her out of the region to relative safety, at great risk to their own lives.

From an Iraqi refugee camp, Murad moved to Germany. She began to speak about what had happened to her, and to the rest of her people – tens of thousands of Yazidis had been killed or displaced. She founded Nadia's Initiative – a non-profit organisation advocating for survivors of sexual violence and the rebuilding of communities in crisis. Just over a year after ISIS had invaded her village, Murad addressed the United Nations about the Yazidi tragedy. Since then, she has continued to speak about the horrors her community still confronts, and the genocide she survived. Relentlessly, she has urged the world to take action and bring ISIS to justice.

In 2018 Nadia Murad won the Nobel Peace Prize for her advocacy work.

Naomi Osaka

Tennis Player
Born 16 October 1997
Japan

Naomi Osaka – born, improbably, in Osaka – is an introvert. However, on tennis courts, her steely focus, candour and confidence shines through. Today, she is a tennis superstar, three-time Grand Slam champion and the world's highest-paid female athlete.

Osaka's father is Haitian, and her mother Japanese. The family moved to New York when she was three – the year she began playing tennis. Growing up, her idol was the great champion Serena Williams. In fact, her father, inspired by the success of the Williams sisters, modelled Naomi and her sister's training after theirs. In 2018, five years after turning pro, Osaka astonished the tennis world by beating Williams for the Women's Singles title at the US Open.

Osaka always intended to play for Japan. In 2019 she relinquished her American citizenship in order to compete as Japanese at the Tokyo Olympics. This decision required some cultural negotiation: Japan does not have a stellar history of accepting biracial citizens with grace. However, Osaka grew up with Japanese traditions as well as Haitian ones, and the girls adopted their mother's surname. (Half-Japanese citizens must retain the Japanese parent's name by law.) Japan's enthusiasm for its new champion is high, and Osaka hopes her vivid cultural presence will encourage greater appreciation of diversity in a country with low rates of intermarriage.

Osaka is also a champion for social justice. In 2020, enraged by the police killing of George Floyd, she marched in Black Lives Matter protests and her Covid-19 protective face masks at the US Open featured the names of victims of race-related police killings. She has also been at the forefront of talking about mental health needs in professional sport. Osaka summarised her position in an interview with *TIME* Magazine, saying, 'It's okay not to be okay, and it's okay to talk about it'.

A rising star, Osaka appears to wield her global celebrity with conscience and care.

Nawal El Saadawi

Doctor, Writer and Women's Rights Activist
27 October 1931 – 21 March 2021
Egypt

When six-year-old Nawal El Saadawi was asked in class to identify herself, she used her mother's name, 'Zeinab', as her surname. The teacher crossed it out, admonishing the girl to use her father's name instead. Upset, El Saadawi observed that her mother's name was considered the less worthy one.

That same year, El Saadawi underwent forced female genital mutilation (FGM). At ten, relatives attempted to marry her off. She resisted, telling her parents she wanted to study.

Young Nawal, then, already had a powerful sense of living under an oppressive patriarchy and was becoming an ardent feminist – although such concepts were a long way from being articulated.

El Saadawi studied medicine in Cairo and New York and was later appointed Director-General of Health Education at Egypt's Ministry of Health, remaining in post until she was expelled for writing her book *Women and Sex* (in which she criticised FGM).

As a psychiatrist, El Saadawi had special insight into the traumas and injustices Egyptian women faced daily. She founded the Arab Women's Solidarity Association, which decried polygamy, inequality and the violation of women's rights. Her writing empowered women but proved unacceptable to Egyptian political and religious authorities. Imprisoned for a time, she wrote *Memoirs from the Women's Prison* on toilet paper, using an eyebrow pencil.

Outspoken and relentless, El Saadawi wrote dozens of books of both fiction and non-fiction, translated into multiple languages. She fled Egypt in 1988 when her life was threatened, and continued to write, speak widely on women's rights and teach at numerous prestigious universities before returning to Cairo in 1996 where she lived until her death in 2021.

Efforts to silence this feminist icon only succeeded in spurring her on. '[They call me] a "wild and dangerous woman"', she has said. 'I speak the truth. And the truth is wild and dangerous.'

Negin Khpalwak

Conductor
Born 2 February 1996
Afghanistan

The year before Negin Khpalwak's birth, the Taliban banned music in Afghanistan – in the streets, at gatherings, even at home. Instruments, cassettes and records were destroyed in attacks on Afghan cultural heritage that was thousands of years old. However, music censorship in Afghanistan was not new. Since 1978, there had been heavy restrictions on music, which was controlled by the communist government.

Khpalwak, born into a Pashtun family, lived in north-eastern Afghanistan. Girls' education in her region was prohibited, but she wanted to study. Her father supported her, and when she was nine he took her to an orphanage in Kabul where she could attend school. Four years later, and having developed a passion for music, Khpalwak applied for admission to the Afghanistan National Institute of Music (ANIM). ANIM was founded in 2010 by a musicologist who had returned to Afghanistan after living in exile for many years. Khpalwak did not tell her family about the application.

The ban on music had been removed when Taliban was brought down in 2001, but in many conservative families, it was still considered sinful. While visiting her family, Khpalwak received news of her acceptance at ANIM. Her mother was shocked; in their region, even boys weren't allowed to study music. Khpalwak's father was once again supportive, although her uncles threatened violence against her, and people warned the family that she would bring them shame. Khpalwak remained courageous, and accepted her place.

Talented and hardworking, Khpalwak learned to play the lute-like robab and the piano. She also studied singing, before becoming Afghanistan's first female conductor. Famously, she lead the all-female orchestra 'Zohra', which was named after the Persian goddess of music. Zohra, founded in 2015, has since performed around the world, from New Delhi to Sydney, Berlin, Davos and New York. Khpalwak made her family proud, achieved her dreams and entered history.

'I will never accept defeat,' she has said. 'I will continue to play music. I do not feel safe, but when people see me and say, "That is Negin Khpalwak", that gives me energy.'

Noor Jehan

Singer and Actor
21 September 1926 – 23 December 2000
Pakistan

The 'Queen of Melody', Noor Jehan, was one of the most influential singers in South Asia, and a beloved actor. Over her fifty-year career, she acted in forty films before becoming a celebrated playback singer (one whose voice is played over actors' lip-syncing). Fluent in several languages, including Hindi, Urdu and Punjabi, she sang an estimated, and staggering, 20,000 songs for films.

Born Allah Rakhi Wasai in then-British India, Noor Jehan's golden voice caught her mother's attention when she was just five years old. Her parents hastened to provide her with training in classical singing from the renowned vocalist Bade Ghulam Ali Khan. As she got older, Noor developed an interest in acting, along with her sisters. The family relocated to Calcutta, where better opportunities awaited. There, the great actor Mukhtar Begum took the sisters under her wing. She introduced them to producers and directors and bestowed the stage name 'Baby Noor Jehan' upon Allah Wasai – presumably an homage to the Mughal empress. Thus, a leading lady was born.

Following the partition of India, Noor Jehan – by now married, and a mother (she would have six children altogether, by two husbands) – moved with her family to the new nation of Pakistan. In 1951 she appeared as the main character in her first Pakistani film. She was also the playback singer and co-director along with her husband, making her the country's first female film director. Her presence in Pakistan shored up the entertainment industry in Lahore, after many other creative talents had left there for Mumbai.

During Pakistan's 1965 war with India, Noor Jehan's patriotic songs, broadcast on the radio, had a profound effect on the morale of Pakistani soldiers. She received numerous awards and honours throughout her lifetime, including Pakistan's national Star of Excellence. In 1982, she returned to India, where she was received by Prime Minister Indira Gandhi.

Oprah Winfrey

Television Host, Actor, CEO and Philanthropist
Born 29 January 1954
United States of America

Oprah Winfrey, known universally just as 'Oprah', began life as 'Orpah'. However, so many people mispronounced her Biblical name that she retained the misnomer.

From 1986 to 2011, Winfrey was watched by millions every week as the host of *The Oprah Winfrey Show* on US television. Through her fame from the hit show, and on account of Winfrey's subsequent ventures – her magazine, film production company and television network – she became the world's first Black female billionaire, and the wealthiest self-made woman in the US.

Winfrey's earthy, tender engagement with talk-show guests, and her immediate emotional connection with audiences – especially women – became more pronounced as she tackled urgent social issues and controversies. One of the most influential people in the world, her book-club recommendations generated best-sellers, and her political endorsements were hotly sought by presidential candidates.

Winfrey was raised by her grandmother in rural Mississippi, in such poverty that her clothes were made from old sacks. She later lived with her mother in an impoverished, dangerous Milwaukee neighbourhood. The harsh circumstances, including repeated sexual abuse from the age of nine, transformed Winfrey into a troubled teenager. She was sent to live with her father in Nashville, and credits him with saving her life. He gave her direction, set strict rules and emphasised her education. Winfrey attended university on a full scholarship and entered the broadcast industry, becoming Nashville's first African American newscaster.

Having taken over a failing Chicago television show as host, she made it immensely popular within a year. It was renamed after her, and, totalling 4,500 episodes and more than forty Emmy television awards, remains the highest-rated talk show ever. Winfrey now enjoys success as the CEO of her own media empire, and oversees numerous charitable foundations disbursing hundreds of millions of dollars to help people in need. In 2013, she received the Presidential Medal of Freedom from Barack Obama.

Oumou Sangaré

Singer/Songwriter
Born 25 February 1968
Mali

From difficult childhood circumstances in her native Bamako, Oumou Sangaré became one of the world's most recognisable musicians. Her life trajectory is thanks to her determination not only to realise her own dreams, but also to empower women through music, giving voice to their lives.

Sangaré's music has its roots in the Wassoulou genre: named after the region, at the junction of Mali, Sierra Leone, Ivory Coast and Guinea, from which it derives. Wassoulou is performed largely by women, and its themes reflect women's realities.

Sangaré was two years old when her father abandoned her pregnant mother Aminata Diakité – a singer who performed at weddings and other occasions – and took a second wife in Ivory Coast. To help support her family, Sangaré left school and began singing in the streets. Later, she joined Aminata, from whom she inherited her musical gifts, working with her at events. She began performing professionally on her own at thirteen and joined a band at sixteen, touring Europe.

Upon her return to Bamako, she began writing her own Wassoulou songs. Sangaré's lyrics, fuelled by her powerful voice, decried the damaging impact of polygamy on women, the pain of child marriage, and other feminist issues. In 1990, she released her first album, *Moussolou* ('Women'). She became a star across Africa, Europe, Asia and, eventually, the US, where she won a Grammy Award. 'The Songbird of Wassoulou' has shared stages with the likes of Baaba Maal, Femi Kuti and Boukman Eksperyans.

For ten years, Sangaré stopped performing internationally to spend more time with her young son. She invested in a hotel in Bamako with a performance space, a farm and other businesses, including an automobile manufacturing enterprise. In 2006, after a decade away, she resumed recording and touring enthusiastically. Her most recent album was released in 2020, and Sangaré continues to sell out venues wherever she performs.

Parveena Ahanger

Human Rights Activist
Born 1958
Kashmir

Parveena Ahanger, known as 'The Iron Lady of Kashmir,' has now been fighting for human rights and justice for over thirty years.

Ahanger was married as a pre-teen. A shy housewife, she lived in Srinagar, Kashmir's largest city. A few years after marriage, she was already a mother of three. But then, tragically, in 1990 her sixteen-year-old son Javed was abducted by Indian soldiers, and became yet another victim of human-rights violations in Kashmir.

India and Pakistan have fought wars over Kashmir since the partition of newly independent India in 1947. In 1948, the United Nations passed a resolution empowering Kashmiris to decide their own fate; however, the conflict endures, severely affecting millions.

Ahanger was uneducated, and rarely left home, but following Javed's disappearance she went to police stations and known torture centres to look for him. She and her husband went to court repeatedly to advance their case, but India's Armed Forces Special Powers Act grants the military immunity from prosecution. This allows the army to act with impunity, including the abduction, detention, rape and killing of Kashmiris. Ahanger and her husband were unable to get any answers – or justice.

Undeterred, Ahanger went from village to village, spreading word about Javed's abduction. People discouraged her; some were too frightened of repercussions to help her search, and some even called Ahanger a bad mother for neglecting her other children. However, along the way, Ahanger also found parents of other disappeared people. In 1994, after years of official indifference, Ahanger gathered a group of these despairing parents and founded the Association of Parents of Disappeared Persons. Through it, she has brought global attention to the psychological trauma, financial insecurity and hopelessness wrought by India's actions in Kashmir.

Ahanger has travelled widely, educating people about what has happened to the Kashmiris. In 2005, she was nominated for the Nobel Peace Prize. In 2017, she was the recipient of the Rafto Prize, a major human rights award; and she featured in the BBC's *100 Women* series in 2019.

Prudence Mabele

HIV and Gender Rights Activist
Born 21 July 1971 – 10 July 2017
South Africa

In 1992, a twenty-one-year-old student named Prudence Mabele became one of the first women in South Africa to openly declare a HIV-positive diagnosis. At the time, HIV/AIDS was shrouded in fear and the stigma and prejudice accompanying such a public disclosure were extremely intense. This was especially true in South Africa, which was preoccupied by its joyful transition from a state of apartheid and was unprepared to face the deadly seriousness of its growing AIDS problem.

After her announcement, Mabele was met with insults, presumptions that she was a sex worker, and expectations that she would soon die. When Mabele's university barred her from continuing her studies in medical technology, fearful that she would infect others, Mabele turned instead to volunteer work and, sadly, struggled with suicidal feelings.

Despite this, in 1996 Mabel founded the Positive Women's Network, offering information and support for HIV-positive women. In 1998, she helped start the Treatment Action Campaign, which fought to make antiretroviral treatment available. In South Africa, official AIDS denialism reached critical proportions after the 1999 election of President Thabo Mbeki, who refused to recognise AIDS as a virus and take realistic measures to combat it. The epidemic surged into the millions. By 2008, when Mbeki left office, nearly 19 per cent of South Africa's population lived with HIV. Mabele, a fearless activist, spoke out against government inaction during this time and fought for treatment access and better services for all affected. She also brought attention to violence against women and the LGBTQ community. She campaigned tirelessly, and even incurred the ire of *sangomas* – traditional healers, of which she was one – when she insisted that Western science should be better integrated into traditional medicine practices.

Mabele died in 2017 from pneumonia-related complications, after living a life conducted with grace, courage and integrity. A truly selfless person who worked to better the lives of those around her, she rose from despair to heroism in incredibly difficult circumstances.

Razia Sultan

Empress
1205 – 1240
India

Sultan Shams ud Din Iltutmish of the Mamluk Dynasty had three sons along with a daughter named Razia, who was his favourite. He didn't discriminate between them according to gender; Razia, like her brothers, received training in warfare and administration.

The sultan chose his son Nasiruddin to succeed him, but sadly the young man died prematurely. As his other sons were more interested in the indulgence of royal pleasures than in leadership, the sultan then passed on the mantle of responsibility to Razia. During Iltutmish's absences from Delhi, he used to leave Razia in charge of the state. She looked after all affairs responsibly and with great capability. Soon, Iltutmish announced her as the official heir apparent.

Unfortunately, the nobility refused to accept being under the rule of a woman. They perceived such a turn of events as an insult. Upon Iltutmish's death, they refused to follow his decree establishing Razia as Sultan, and instead appointed her half-brother Raknuddin Firuz Shah. Ruknuddin soon revealed himself as a terrible choice, and in fact it was his mother who managed the running of the state. Months into his reign, he and his mother were both assassinated, and Razia Sultan ascended.

She adopted masculine attire in her court, and on the battlefield. She also refused to be called 'Sultana': the word denoted a wife or mistress of the Sultan. She believed in her supremacy as ruler and took the title of 'Sultan'.

Although her reign was short, Razia Sultan indeed to be a great leader. She cared deeply about the empire and her subjects and was popular with them. She expanded the state's territory, fostered peace and prosperity, founded research centres and public libraries and patronised religious studies, science, philosophy and literature.

Courageous, just and generous, Razia Sultan was the only female ruler to sit on the throne of Delhi.

Rigoberta Menchú

Human Rights Activist
Born 9 January 1959
Guatemala

Being a member of the resistance movement in Guatemala during its brutal civil war (1960–96), especially as a woman from a poor, Indigenous family, required courage. Rigoberta Menchú possessed that courage in great abundance.

Menchú, born into a family of K'iche' Maya peasants, had witnessed the oppression of her people by the military since childhood. The war – properly termed a genocide – saw 200,000 Guatemalans killed and over 1 million displaced. Maya peoples suffered discrimination, land confiscation, malnutrition, sexual violence and murder. Four hundred Maya villages were annihilated.

Menchú's father was an activist with the Committee for Peasant Unity, Guatemala's first Indigenous-led national labour organisation. Menchú followed in her father's footsteps, joining the Committee for Peasant Unity in 1979 and becoming a member of its National Coordinating Committee seven years later. Tragically, her brother and mother were tortured and killed by the army soon afterwards. Her father also died in this period, during a fire at the Spanish embassy in Guatemala City. Peasants protesting injustice had occupied the building, until security forces stormed it and the fatal fire broke out.

Menchú escaped to Mexico in 1981, as tens of thousands of Maya people later did. In exile, she continued to organise resistance against the Guatemalan genocide, which she considered an extension of colonial exploitation. In 1983, her book I, Rigoberta Menchú was published, bringing global attention to this 'Silent Holocaust'. Working with numerous international and local organisations, she became a leading representative of Indigenous and women's rights around the world. Menchú has received many international awards for her brave work, including the 1992 Nobel Peace Prize. Not only was Menchú the first Indigenous recipient, she was also the youngest at the time.

Menchú was Presidential Goodwill Ambassador for the 1996 peace accords in Guatemala. In 2007 and 2011, she stood for presidential election herself. She did not win, but her activism for political and economic equality, human rights and climate change action continues.

Rosa Parks

Civil Rights Activist
4 February 1913 – 24 October 2005
United States of America

Rosa Parks was an activist in the Civil Rights Movement. She is best known for the bus incident in 1955, when she resisted segregation on a bus in Montgomery, Alabama, leading to a 381-day bus boycott. It was a courageous stand, but it was not the first time Parks had stood up against racial injustice, and it would certainly not be the last.

Born in Alabama and raised by her mother and grandparents, as a child Rosa walked to school every day because buses were for whites only. Education was racially segregated at the time, and Rosa's teachers lacked the adequate resources to deliver their pupils a proper education. Rosa eventually dropped out of high school to care for her mother and grandmother who were unwell, working as a seamstress to support them.

Throughout her life, Parks dealt with racism, bigotry and sexual harassment from white people. But she never stayed quiet, whatever the cost. In 1943, she joined the National Association for the Advancement of Coloured People, and soon became the elected secretary of the Montgomery chapter. As part of this activist role, Parks investigated murders, hate crimes and attacks on the African American community. This was gruelling frontline work. In one such case, a woman named Recy Taylor was raped by six white men in Alabama. Parks travelled there to investigate the case. She set up the Committee for Equal Justice for Mrs Recy Taylor, a group which spread awareness of the case and gained further support for the victim.

The Montgomery bus incident became the pivotal moment in desegregating the public transport system in the USA. Parks stood up for what was right, even though she knew it would cause her to be arrested and fired from her job. Parks had been saying 'no' to the powers that kept African Americans oppressed for years, but after she was arrested, she became recognised as the international icon of resistance to racial segregation that she is known as today.

Sanmao

Travel Writer
Born 26 March 1943
Taiwan

After failing a maths test, Chen Mao-ping's teacher paraded her around school with two black zeroes drawn around her eyes. After this incident, Chen – an avid reader whose devotion to books caused her to neglect some other areas of her studies – preferred home-schooling. Later, taking the pen name 'Sanmao' (after a character created by comics artist Zhen Leping), she would make the world her classroom.

Sanmao was born in Chongqing, China. In 1948, with the Communists rising to power, her family moved to Taiwan. Sanmao's father educated her at home, and also hired other teachers. Her art teacher, who called herself 'Echo', nurtured Sanmao's expressive gifts and inspired her pupil to adopt the same name. In years to come, many young girls would rename themselves 'Echo' and mothers would also give this name to their daughters – in honour of Sanmao.

In 1967, feeling constricted by Taiwanese society, Sanmao set off a journey to the US and Europe. She learned German in Germany and Spanish in Spain and studied at the University of Madrid. In 1973, she married José María Quero, who had loved her from afar for years. He quit his career as an engineer to become her travel partner, and together they sojourned in the Sahara, following Sanmao's dream to become the first woman to cross this mysterious desert, which she called her 'dream lover'.

Stories of the Sahara, Sanmao's first book, is a collection of travel essays. It was reprinted three times in the first six weeks after it was published, and thirty reprints followed. Today, it has sold more than 10 million copies. Sanmao's thirst for learning by travelling took her in total to fifty-nine countries. She went on to write nineteen more books and her writing became a source of inspiration for Taiwanese and Chinese readers – especially women.

In 1991, several years after her beloved husband José María Quero died, Sanmao tragically committed suicide. Her books continue to be read in many languages by readers all around the world.

Serena Williams

Tennis Player
Born 26 September 1981
United States of America

Iconic athletes who consistently dominate a sport over several years are rare. For women's tennis, that athlete is Serena Williams. Her professional record of twenty-three Grand Slam championships is unequalled by any man or woman. Her dynamic style, explosive forehands and backhands and unreturnable serves have earned her numerous other records, too. She is also one of the world's highest-earning athletes.

The making of Williams – and her older sister Venus, also considered one of the greatest female tennis players of all time – is legendary. Their father began their training from a very early age with the intention of raising champions. Serena Williams was just four when she first picked up a racket. The girls played on poorly maintained public courts in their tough Los Angeles neighbourhood, where gangs, guns and poverty were common. They were home-schooled, allowing them to focus on tennis, but as they got older, they skipped tournaments to prioritise schoolwork.

At eighteen, Serena won the US Open, her first Grand Slam. Throughout her career she has come back time and time again from losing sets, as well as from injuries, health scares, surgery and burnout, to win championship titles. In 2017, she won the Australian Open while pregnant. Since giving birth she has continued to make the finals, semi-finals and quarterfinals of Grand Slams, regularly.

Tennis remains among the whitest of professional sports, and the Williams sisters contended with racism and sexism throughout the years from journalists, umpires, crowds and competitors. Serena's style has been construed as 'too aggressive' (never an issue for male players); and her body was criticised as 'too masculine', affecting her confidence – briefly. Yet after her 1999 US Open triumph, Williams realised that her powerful body was an instrument of her strong will. Both propelled her to victory.

She has never looked back.

Shirin Ebadi

Lawyer and Human Rights Activist

Born 21 June 1947

Iran

Shirin Ebadi's father was a devoted lawyer, and she fell in love with the law as well. She completed her degree at the University of Tehran, later becoming a judge. In 1971, during her judgeship, she obtained a doctorate. Ambitious, hardworking and brilliant, she was appointed a Chief Magistrate in 1975.

Following the 1979 Islamic Revolution, Ebadi was demoted to clerk; the new theocracy held that Islam didn't allow women to be judges. Ebadi, who had grown up in a Muslim household with parents who taught her about Islam and never discriminated between their daughters and sons, found this unacceptable. Realising that the new regime was misrepresenting Islamic values, she applied for early retirement and left in protest. For years, she was prohibited from obtaining a law licence. During this time, she wrote many books and papers on human rights.

When Ebadi was re-admitted to the profession, she went into private practice, taking on controversial political and human rights cases, all *pro bono*. Some of her most important cases involved her defence of leaders of the Baha'i faith, which is the most persecuted religious minority in Iran. She estimates that she and her team took on 6,000 cases without charge. The government saw her as a threat, and imprisoned her. However, with international pressure, the prison sentence and bar on practising law was reduced to a fine. Still, Ebadi and her loved ones were watched, and constantly in danger; there were reports of an assassination order issued by the intelligence director himself.

In 2003, Ebadi received a Nobel Peace Prize for advocating for democracy and human rights – the first Muslim to win the Peace Prize, and the only Iranian to win a Nobel.

Having left Iran to attend a conference before the 2009 presidential election, Ebadi was prevented from returning on account of restrictions imposed against activists and a crackdown by the government that saw her colleagues arrested, and protestors killed. She now lives in exile in the UK but has never stopped fighting for the rights of Iranians.

Shirin Neshat

Visual Artist
Born 26 March 1957
Iran and United States of America

Shirin Neshat's work centres on oppositions – religious/secular; East/West; masculine/feminine. She hopes the people who see her work do not respond to 'some heavy political statement, but something that really touches them on the most emotional level'. This sentiment sits alongside her view of her own art which, in Neshat's own words, 'is concerned with tyranny, dictatorship, oppression and political injustice. Although I don't consider myself an activist ... my art ... is an expression of protest, a cry for humanity.'

At seventeen, Neshat's father sent her to attend university in the US, where her sister was also enrolled in higher education. Neshat was unfamiliar with American cultural expectations and felt isolated. She was studying Fine Arts at the University of California when the Iranian Revolution erupted in 1979. Iran's relationship with the US deteriorated rapidly, and Neshat didn't know if she would see the rest of her family again.

In 1990, visiting Iran became possible, and Neshat reunited with her loved ones. Her joy alternated with the shock of returning to an unrecognisable country. Post-revolutionary Iran, and especially the lives of women, had been drastically altered. This experience inspired Neshat's first major works, from the *Women of Allah* series (featuring photographs of veiled women with overlaid text) to video installations such as *Turbulent*, winner of the 1999 Venice Biennale.

Neshat's work attracted global attention: here was someone, it was felt, who could describe what it was like to be an Iranian woman. Her video work explored history, Iranian socio-politics and women in Iran – but they were not filmed there. Her 'Iranian' scenes have been shot in Morocco, Turkey, Mexico and elsewhere. Neshat's art is too threatening for Iranian authorities, and she has been in exile since 1996.

Neshat has fought two battles: against the unreal perceptions of Iran in the West, and against the Iranian regime itself. In both cases, art is her weapon.

Shirley Coleen

Humanitarian and Activist
22 November 1921 – 28 April 1998
Australia

Mum Shirl – born Colleen Shirley Perry Smith – was an Aboriginal woman of Wiradjuri descent, born in New South Wales. Schooling was difficult for her as she had epilepsy. At the time, not many people understood the condition, and no proper treatment existed for it. As a result, she was taught at home, by her grandfather. She couldn't read or write, but knew approximately sixteen Aboriginal languages.

Mum Shirl and her family eventually moved to a low-income, majority-Aboriginal neighbourhood in Sydney. When her brother Laurie was arrested for theft, she visited him in prison and connected with other inmates there, as well. After Laurie's release, she continued to visited other inmates regularly to comfort them. When the guards asked what her relationship to an inmate was, she would reply she was his mother – hence the name by which she became known, 'Mum Shirl'. Over the years, she visited thousands of inmates.

Mum Shirl was a compassionate person who cared deeply about people's well-being. She opened her home to orphans and abandoned kids, caring for more than sixty children over her lifetime. She also helped women facing domestic violence, and people suffering from alcoholism and unemployment.

Mum Shirl was a founding member of many different kinds of organisations that served Aboriginal communities, such as the Aboriginal Medical Service, Aboriginal Legal Service, Aboriginal Housing Company, Aboriginal Black Theatre, and others. As an activist, she was very involved in Australia's civil rights and Aboriginal land rights movements, calling for racial equality and bringing attention to issues and injustices confronted by the country's Aboriginal peoples. She was awarded Member of the British Empire in 1977, Member of the Order of Australia in 1985, and Aborigine of the Year 1990 for her work. A few months before her death, the National Trust recognised her as an Australian National Living Treasure.

Mum Shirl was not a woman of great means, but she shared whatever she had. She dedicated her life to helping others, changing thousands of lives through love, generosity, care and determination.

Simone Biles

Gymnast
Born 14 March 1997
United States of America

When Simone Biles pioneered a very difficult new routine at the 2019 Gymnastics World Championship – a 'double-double beam dismount' (two flips and two twists, now called simply 'the Biles') – the judges rated it lower than expected, explaining that they did not want to encourage her competitors to risk danger by attempting to equal it. Such is Simone Biles's redefinition of gymnastics.

Biles, who has won over thirty medals in the World Championships and the Olympics, is the most-decorated female gymnast in history. She has set many records. She is the first American female gymnast to win a world medal in every event and the first female gymnast to win three consecutive world championships (she's actually won five). She is often referred to as the greatest gymnast of all time.

As a child in Columbus, Ohio, Biles was placed into foster care alongside her three siblings. Their mother, an alcoholic and drug abuser, was unable to care for them. When the children's grandparents learned of the situation, they adopted Biles and her younger sister and the other two children were adopted by an aunt. Biles was six years old.

That year, she was signed up for gymnastics classes, and started competing when she was seven. Everyone could discern her powerful talent: Biles's coach observed that she could master a new move in three days; other gymnasts require months, or even years.

Biles trained hard, undertaking home-schooling to accommodate her schedule. Too young for the 2012 Olympics, she trained for thirty-five hours a week for the next four years. At the 2016 Olympics she won four gold medals and one bronze, becoming the first African American female all-around world champion. In 2021, after withdrawing from some of the competitions at the Tokyo Olympics, Biles opened up about her mental health. She has received wide support for her courage in doing so.

When compared to other legendary Olympians, Biles replied: 'I'm not the next Usain Bolt or Michael Phelps. I'm the first Simone Biles.'

Sonia Sotomayor

Supreme Court Justice
Born 25 June 1954
United States of America

The first Hispanic and Latina justice – and third female justice – to serve on the US's highest court wanted to be a detective as a girl. However, influenced by television's Perry Mason (a defence lawyer who favoured 'hopeless' cases, yet always won the day), Sonia Sotomayor became attracted to a career in law. She has recalled a prosecutor on the show declaring that losing cases was tolerable if defendants were proven innocent. At that point, she realised how important judges were in the justice system: 'The guy who made the decision to dismiss the case [exonerating the defendant] was the judge. That was what I was going to be.'

Born and raised in New York's tough South Bronx neighbourhood, Sotomayor is a proud New Yorker of Puerto Rican heritage. Her father died when she was nine. To cope with the loss, she spent hours reading at a local library. Her mother worked two jobs and pushed Sotomayor and her brother relentlessly to focus on their education. It paid off: after attending Princeton on a scholarship, graduating with highest honours, Sotomayor studied law at Yale.

In 1980, as an assistant district attorney in Manhattan, Sotomayor prosecuted serious crimes such as assault, murder, police brutality and child pornography. After several years in private practice during which her pro bono work for socially conscious organisations attracted the attention of senior politicians, she was appointed judge to two important higher courts. Then, in 2009, President Barack Obama nominated her to the Supreme Court.

Sotomayor has been targeted and her personal safety threatened as a result of her work and reputation. Throughout her career, Sotomayor has upheld abortion rights, freedom of speech and property rights. As a liberal Justice on a majority-conservative Court, she has defended healthcare and dissented against police searches, as well as against President Donald Trump's infamous 'travel ban' restricting entry into the US by people from Muslim countries.

Sophia Duleep Singh

Suffragette
8 August 1876 – 22 August 1948
United Kingdom

Sophia Duleep Singh was the daughter of the last Sikh *maharaja*, goddaughter of Queen Victoria, and a style icon keen on cycling, photography and attending lavish parties. With such a biography, Singh might be considered an unlikely social activist, much less a hero of the women's suffrage movement in Britain.

Born in Norfolk and orphaned at the age of seventeen, the shy princess became resident at Hampton Court Palace and a socialite under British government surveillance. However, during a lapse in its vigilance, she made a covert trip to India in 1903 – and to the territory once ruled by her grandfather's empire. On a second trip in 1907, she witnessed the impoverishment and suffering of Indians under the British Raj. Singh befriended independence activists, and turned ardently against British rule.

Her awakening found a parallel when she returned: women in Britain were protesting furiously for the right to vote, and she joined the movement with great vigour, becoming a leading suffragette. Singh endorsed anarchy, withheld her taxes and even – controversially – sold politically progressive newspapers outside her palace residence. She funded suffragette groups in the UK as well as supporting women's suffrage in other countries and took direct action herself: once jumping in front of the prime minister's car with a placard advocating universal suffrage. On 'Black Friday', 18 November 1910, Singh marched on Parliament with movement founder Emmeline Pankhurst and hundreds of other women. Police on the day countered them with violence and sexual assault.

Singh's commitment to the advancement of women never wavered, but her social activism was broad and impassioned: during the First World War, she volunteered as a nurse, tending to wounded Indian soldiers evacuated from the frontlines.

In 1918, women over thirty obtained the right to vote, extending to women aged twenty-one and over in 1928. Singh lived to see both occasions, towards which she had dedicated so much.

Sylvia Tamale

Lawyer, Academic and Feminist Activist
Born 2 April 1962
Uganda

Sylvia Tamale's work is essential reading for African perspectives on gender, feminism and sexuality – and associated laws and rights. The Ugandan academic and activist was the first female Dean of the Law Faculty at Makerere University. She has worked on theory and jurisprudence underlying patriarchal oppression across Africa today. She argues that resurgent 'cultural, economic and religious fundamentalisms' safeguarding male power and privilege must be challenged, and challenges them directly herself throughout her work.

Tamale strives to transform Ugandan lives, from the young students who attend her lectures to her own family and strangers in public spaces. She has also successfully fought Ugandan laws discriminating against women in cases of divorce, adultery and inheritance. At Makerere in 2018, she headed a committee examining sexual harassment on and off campus, which resulted in stricter policies being established.

Tamale has won several awards for defending the rights of marginalised groups such as sex workers, homosexuals and refugees. In 2003, she was named Worst Woman of the Year by Uganda's largest daily newspaper, which portrayed her as a degenerate for recommending to the government's Equal Opportunities Commission that the legal term 'minorities' be broadened to include LGBT people. Tamale's response to the newspaper was to declare the title 'a badge of honour'.

A graduate of Makerere University's law school, with an MA from Harvard and a PhD from the University of Minnesota, Tamale has published several books and articles on Afrofeminism and African sexuality and politics, such as *African Sexualities: A Reader* (2011).

As a feminist, Tamale strives for inclusivity, inviting men into the discourse as well as religious women and women of different political persuasions. 'I am always uplifted by ... the Universal Declaration of Human Rights,' Tamale has written. 'All human beings are born free and equal in dignity and rights.'

Tawakkol Karman

Journalist and Human Rights Activist
Born 7 February 1979
Yemen

In 2005, civil war in Yemen was still a decade away. It was five years before The Arab Spring and the authority of Yemen's long-entrenched dictator, Ali Abdullah Saleh, was secure. In this climate, Tawakkol Karman co-founded an organisation called, provocatively, Women Journalists Without Chains, which called for freedom of expression and removal of press restrictions.

Becoming the public face of dissent in Yemen at that time required courage: harassment and death threats were routine for those who opposed the regime. Moreover Karman, a journalist herself, demanded more rights for women in a predominantly patriarchal society. She decried and rallied against female illiteracy, malnutrition, lack of access to education, early marriage and controls on movement.

As the Arab Spring was gathering momentum, Karman organised weekly protests calling for an end to Saleh's rule. She insisted firearms, which were widely available in Yemen, should be left at home, and encouraged only peaceful protests. Despite being arrested and detained multiple times, Karman persisted with her activities as the crowds grew. 'The combination of dictatorship, corruption, poverty and unemployment has created this revolution,' she explained. 'It's like a volcano. Injustice and corruption are exploding while opportunities for a good life are coming to an end.' Abroad, Karman lobbied the UN and met with US officials in an attempt to ensure that Saleh was held accountable for his actions, despite their reluctance. Nevertheless, he was deposed in 2011, the same year that Karman was awarded the Nobel Peace Prize, making her the first Yemeni, Arab woman and, at the time, the youngest, Laureate. She only learned that she had won the prize from a friend, as she was out organising protests.

Called the 'Mother of the Revolution' by many Yemenis, Karman fled to Istanbul in Turkey when the rebel Houthis conquered the capital city of Sana'a in 2014. She continues to travel widely, speaking and writing on the situation in Yemen.

Taytu Betul

Empress and Warrior
1851 – 1918
Ethiopia

Unusually for a woman of her society, Taytu Betul was educated and able to write and read in Amharic. This is surprising, as there is no record that Betul attended school, and it is likely that, from the age of ten, preparations for her first of five marriages began.

A woman of many talents and interests, Betul composed poetry, played a stringed instrument called the *begena* and had a reputation as a formidable chess player. The most well-documented part of her life began after she married Emperor Menelik II, her fifth husband. She had no children with any of her husbands – something of a scandal, as motherhood was considered a woman's primary role in life. Betul never abided by society's rules, however. As Empress, she played a valuable role, advising the emperor on all political matters. She was suspicious, in an age of imperialist invasions, of foreigners visiting Ethiopia to seek government contracts. Betul never wanted to compromise Ethiopian heritage or values.

She founded Addis Ababa as the empire's capital, and, alongside her husband, laid the foundations for medical care, postal services, wool production, the railway, the tax system and more. Under this powerful couple, Ethiopia advanced into modernity.

The Battle of Adwa was a historic moment in Betul's legacy. Menelik II signed the Treaty of Wuchale with Italy in 1889, strengthening the relationship between the two nations. But Italy had other plans, and tried to make Ethiopia a colony. The treaty had Amharic and Italian versions. An article in the latter – absent from the Amharic version – declared Ethiopia a protectorate of Italy. War ensued.

Betul was present on the frontlines, and led Ethiopian troops to victory against Italian forces with strategic brilliance and courage. Italy's defeat was a momentous event; Ethiopia had defended its sovereignty, and became an inspiration for African freedom.

In the early 1900s, when Menelik II fell seriously ill, Betul took all the decisions affecting the empire. After his death, she retired from her duties and lived out her days in peace.

Tebello Nyokong

Chemist
Born 20 October 1951
South Africa

Tebello Nyokong is a chemist and a university professor. She was born in Lesotho, her mother's homeland. Her father had a strong and positive influence on his children, motivating them to pursue their schooling even though the family was of modest means. He believed that education was the key to ending apartheid. Having studied to sixth grade himself, he cared deeply that his children should progress further than he had.

One of Nyokong's childhood ambitions was to own her own pair of shoes. She worked as a shepherd, attending school on alternate days. She was discouraged when she showed interest in the sciences. 'Science is difficult for girls,' she was told. 'You cannot handle it.' Thus deterred, Nyokong took art courses instead – until a teacher inspired to switch to science after all.

Nyokong wasn't sure about attending university but went to the University of Lesotho because a friend of hers applied. She fell in love with chemistry and went on to obtain a BSc in Chemistry and Biology. After receiving a Canadian International Development Agency scholarship, she would obtain her MA in Canada as well as her PhD, in 1987.

All that was challenging for a mother of two who had to leave her family behind. In Canada, cultural differences and feelings of isolation got to her at times. But Nyokong was there to acquire knowledge. She researched alternative cancer treatments to chemotherapy, developing a drug that can be combined with photodynamic therapy: that is, injected into the patient and activated by light. She also received a fellowship to continue her studies in the United States. When she returned to Africa, she began lecturing in Medicinal Chemistry and Nanotechnology at Rhodes University, where she is now a Distinguished Professor.

Nyokong has also invested her time training a new generation of chemists, and in programmes to supply unused lab equipment to local schools, to attract more young people to study science. The recipient of many awards and honours, she has paved the way for other women in science, technology, engineering and mathematics.

Tererai Trent

Academic and Humanitarian
Born 1965
Zimbabwe

———————

Tererai Trent grew up in rural present-day Zimbabwe. When she was eleven, her father married her off. Before she was eighteen, she had given birth to four children, losing one from the inability to nourish them all. Her lot was not uncommon. Her mother and grandmother were child brides, too.

When a woman named Jo Luck, who headed a development organisation, visited Trent's village, she asked Trent what her dreams were – something no one had ever done before. Yet Trent had a ready answer: to obtain an education. Poverty was common in many parts of colonial Zimbabwe (then called Rhodesia), and boys' education took priority over girls'. Trent had tried to augment her own primary education, which had lasted less than a year, by borrowing her brother's schoolbooks.

Luck replied: '*Tinogona*. It is achievable.' Trent's mother further encouraged her, advising her to write her dreams down. Trent recorded four dreams on a piece of paper, sealed the paper in a tin can, and buried it. The dreams were to live abroad, and to obtain a BA, MA and PhD.

Trent took correspondence courses for eight years, persisting after failing several times. She wanted to break the cycle of poverty and education deprivation and give her daughters different futures.

Trent worked for aid organisations and was accepted to university in the US. Life there was difficult, but with support from her community, she persevered and earned her BA in 2001. In 2009 she received her PhD, thus fulfilling all four dreams.

Trent became a professor at Drexel University in Pennsylvania, conducted research on HIV prevention in Africa, wrote best-selling memoirs, advocated for girls' education on global platforms and started a foundation for children's education in Africa. She also rebuilt the primary school in her village with support from Oprah Winfrey, who revealed that Trent was her all-time favourite TV guest.

Dr Tererai Trent has helped educate thousands of children in Zimbabwe, while inspiring millions around the world.

Theresa Kachindamoto

Senior Chief
Born 1959
Malawi

Education is a right, but many girls in Malawi have none. However, thanks to her father, Theresa Kachindamoto left her village for schooling. Some years later, while working as a secretary at a college in the city of Zomba, she observed girls being educated and planning careers, which gave her immense joy.

When her father died, Kachindamoto was asked to replace him as one of Malawi's 300 tribal leaders, taking over his role as senior chief of the district of Dedza, overseeing more than 900,000 people. She accepted the role reluctantly.

One day in the village, a young girl with a baby on her back caught Kachindamoto's attention. She learned that the girl was a mother at only thirteen. To her horror, Kachindamoto discovered that girls as young as twelve were being married off, often after being taken to 'initiation camps' when they reached puberty, to learn how to please men and be submissive. At the end of this 'cleansing' ritual, the initiates were brought to men who were paid by the village to have sexual intercourse with them.

Malawi had one of the highest rates of child marriage in the world. Fifty per cent of women were married before their eighteenth birthday. Families married off daughters because they could not afford to keep them. The girls could face domestic violence, rape and pregnancy after marriage, and risked contracting HIV – all of which resulted too often in trauma, health issues and early death.

Kachindamoto began sharing her plan to eradicate child marriage. Some chiefs became upset, and even warned her that her life would be endangered for threatening their traditions. Yet Kachindamoto's mission was unwavering. She also ensured that girls who would otherwise have been married, received schooling, and has, at times, paid for their education herself. In 2015, Malawi passed a law that made marriage illegal before the age of eighteen. Kachindamoto is known as the 'Terminator' for ending more than a thousand child marriages to date.

Tu Youyou

Scientist
Born 30 December 1930
China

Tu Youyou is a Chinese chemist. Her breakthroughs in the fields of tropical medicine have saved millions of lives across Asia, Africa, South America and beyond.

When Youyou was just sixteen years old, she contracted tuberculosis. Her long illness meant that she was unable to attend school for two years. During her time of sickness and recovery, Youyou resolved to pursue a career in medicine, because she wanted to find cures and help heal others. With this goal in mind, she obtained a degree in Pharmacology from Beijing Medical College and began her career at the Academy of Traditional Chinese Medicine.

Youyou's most significant breakthrough is in her work to combat malaria. During the Vietnam War, many, many soldiers died from this tropical disease, which is spread by mosquitos carrying the infection. President Ho Chi Minh of Vietnam turned to the Chinese government for help. In response to the plea, in 1967 the Chinese government launched Project 523 to look for a cure for malaria. Two years later, Youyou, now a mother of two, was made project lead. When she took over managing the work, more than 240,000 compounds had been tested and proved unsuccessful in the fight against the disease.

Youyou's research involved a number of approaches, including looking at ancient Chinese texts and medical treatises. It occurred to her that perhaps the compounds were being destroyed on account of the high boiling temperatures used during the experiments. She tried another form of compound extraction and made a breakthrough. Rodent trials showed positive results. Youyou and two of her colleagues volunteered themselves for human trials, which were also successful. Their discovery, called Artemisinin-based combination therapy, is used to help millions of malaria patients around the world today.

Tu Youyou won the Nobel Prize in Physiology or Medicine in 2015 for her brilliant work. She became the first Chinese citizen to win the Nobel Prize in this category, and the first woman from China ever to receive a Nobel Prize.

Umm Kulthum

Singer
6 May 1904 – 3 February 1975
Egypt

Umm Kulthum (Fatima) Ibrahim al-Sayyid El-Beltagi was a singer from Egypt and a social phenomenon. As the youngest daughter of an imam who performed religious songs at local weddings, her upbringing was an unconventional start to a life of stardom. After hearing her father practising one day, Umm Kulthum asked him if she could sing with his small, all-male, group. Soon after, Umm Kulthum stood in for her brother at a public performance when he fell ill. Word spread about her enchanting voice and she began to receive invitations from nearby villages to sing, sometimes walking for miles to reach a venue.

Umm Kulthoum's early concerts were controversial. Some members of the community disapproved of gatherings for entertainment (which occasionally included drinking alcohol). Umm Kulthum's father worried about her safety and reputation to such an extent that, during her teens, he made her wear a boy's coat and a traditional Bedouin headscarf whenever she performed. In the 1930s, Umm Kulthoum left the village where she was born for cosmopolitan Cairo, where her reputation grew and grew. Her voice was a contralto, the lowest for a female voice, and was so powerful that she performed without a microphone. Her concerts lasted for hours. Audiences regularly requested encores of their favourite lines, with the result that a single song could last ninety minutes. Because of the way she changed scales and altered the emphasis in a phrase, it was said she never sang the same line twice.

Umm Kulthum recorded around 300 songs over her sixty-year career. For forty years, she broadcast a live concert on the first Thursday of every month, with the result that she became an unmatchable, global icon of the twentieth century, and a household name across the Middle East. She embodied pan-Arab unity, and her songs of love, longing and loss are still played in taxis, radios and cafes across the Arab world today.

Wangari Maathai

Biologist, Environmentalist and Activist
1 April 1940 – 25 September 2011
Kenya

Wangari Maathai is recognised internationally for her relentless struggle for human rights and environmental conservation. She was born and raised in the village of Ihithe, Kenya. It was rare for a girl of her background even to attend school; going on to university was an extraordinary achievement. But Maathai received a scholarship to study in the US, where she earned her BA and MA in Biology. She later obtained a PhD after studying in Germany and Kenya, becoming the first woman in East and Central Africa to earn a doctorate degree.

Maathai then became a professor of veterinary anatomy. At the same time, she was a member of various grassroots organisations tackling social problems, especially for rural women, who struggled to find basic resources such as firewood, food and water. Maathai recognised the connection between poverty and the environment, describing them as two sides of the same coin. In 1977, she established the Green Belt Movement to focus on environmental conservation and community development.

Maathai constantly confronted the government, which controlled land and resources. When, in 1989, Nairobi's Uhuru Park was to be destroyed to make way for a sixty-storey building, Maathai and her supporters protested, making national headlines. The investors pulled out of the project, and Uhuru Park was saved. In December 2002, she was elected to parliament.

Maathai worked tirelessly to combat deforestation, fight for human rights and agitate for a more democratic Kenyan government. She has won countless international prizes for her work on sustainable development, peace and democracy, including, in 2004, the Nobel Peace Prize. Asked what the connection was between the environment and peace, she replied: 'When you look at the world, what do people fight over? They are fighting for water ... for land ... [for] resources.' She believed preserving the environment and equitably distributing resources is the key to decreasing poverty and fostering world peace. The Green Belt Movement has planted over 50 million trees, created jobs and inspired millions to pay closer attention to the environment.

Wangechi Mutu

Visual Artist
Born 22 June 1972
Kenya

Wangechi Mutu trained as both a sculptor and an anthropologist. Her visionary, haunting and utterly compelling artwork testifies to her close interest in different cultures. Never restricting herself to a single medium or theme, Mutu has made collages, films, installations and sculptures exploring gender, colonialism and race, often centred on Black women's bodies. Her Afrofuturist worldscapes confront the pain and discourse of our times.

Born in Nairobi, Mutu's father was a businessman and her mother was a natural healer. Mutu completed her schooling at UWC Wales and then obtained a BFA from Cooper Union in New York, followed by an MFA in sculpture from Yale University in 2000. She had begun to settle as an artist in New York when the 9/11 terrorist attacks occurred. Mutu watched as fear became widespread and a new cloud of racism set in, causing Americans to view foreigners with suspicion. Her art allowed her to release her anxiety. She created beautiful collages using paints, inks and cut-outs from magazines, and in 2003 she was invited to take part in a group exhibition with a dozen other artists – a turning point for her.

In 2018 the Metropolitan Museum of Art asked Mutu to create sculptures for the exterior niches of its façade, which had been unoccupied for more than 110 years. She made caryatids – human figures that traditionally support architectural features – but far from the Classical kind, instead sculpting women in active poses, without having them bear anyone or anything.

Today, Mutu has exhibited across the world, as an artist attuned to some of the most complex nuances of the twenty-first century. She is also the founder of Africa's Out!, a platform to 'advance radical change through the power of art and activism', supporting artists and initiatives from Africa and the Diaspora 'celebrating creative expression', beginning with LGBTQI rights.

Wilma Mankiller

Activist and Principal Chief of the Cherokee Nation
18 November 1945 – 6 April 2010
United States of America

Wilma Mankiller grew up in Oklahoma Cherokee territory. She and her ten siblings spoke Cherokee at home and were taught traditions by tribal elders. They lived in extreme poverty, steeped in living conditions she would later do so much to change.

The family moved to San Francisco, living in troubled neighbourhoods and struggling financially. Alienated from tribal ways and facing racism and discrimination, young Wilma found school difficult, but San Francisco's cultural diversity and political ferment transformed her into a feminist and activist.

Mankiller married and had two daughters, but her husband discouraged her personal growth. Increasing dedication to Native American issues pushed her to pursue university education. She obtained a divorce and began working in Oakland as a social worker – later returning with her daughters to Oklahoma to work for the Cherokee Nation. There she developed programmes for healthcare and child and elder welfare, and secured community infrastructure redevelopment grants.

In 1983, shortly after surviving a near-lethal car accident and being treated for (unrelated) myasthenia gravis, Mankiller was elected Deputy Chief, running with the tribe's Principal Chief Ross Swimmer. They overcame vicious sexism to become a successful team, but doubts persisted even as Mankiller presided over the tribal council. Yet her policies were effective, and when Swimmer moved into federal politics, Mankiller replaced him as Chief. She held the position for a decade and was re-elected twice.

Progressive, farsighted and focused on cultural pride, Mankiller emphasised economic growth and social programmes. Tribal revenue was invested in health clinics, job training and other forms of self-improvement. Infant mortality dropped, and educational enrolment and employment grew – as did the budget, which doubled to $150 million by 1995, when she resigned because of ill health.

'I want to be remembered as the person who helped us restore faith in ourselves,' Mankiller said.

Yayoi Kusama

Artist
Born 22 March 1929
Japan

Millions of people worldwide have visited exhibitions of Yayoi Kusama's work. A conceptual artist known for her paintings, sculptures, installations, fashion and more, Kusama moved from Japan to New York in 1957, and became a leading figure in the game-changing Pop Art movement of the 1960s.

In the 1970s, that all came to a halt for Kusama. Her career did not revive for nearly two decades.

Kusama has been open about her mental health issues. The youngest daughter of a prosperous family, she began experiencing vivid hallucinations at ten years old: flowers spoke to her and multiplied rapidly, engulfing her, as did flashes of light, auras, swirling patterns and dots. Growing up, Kusama also had a complicated family life. Her abusive mother compelled her to spy on her serially unfaithful father and discouraged Kusama's artistic activity – often destroying her work.

Kusama – who credits making art with saving her from suicidal despair – is known for obsessional works inspired directly by her visions as well as her neurotic disgust toward sexuality. Her childhood trauma – family-related, but also stemming from forced labour in factories during the Second World War – has been transmuted alchemically into colourful, dynamic, fantastical art, often featuring polka dot-saturated 'infinity nets', that has brought joy to viewers who are frequently unaware of her history. Her art is 'inextricably connected' to her mental illness, she has said. 'By translating hallucinations and fear … into paintings, I have been trying to cure my disease.'

Kusama returned to Japan in 1973, and has been living voluntarily and peacefully at a psychiatric facility since 1977. Since the late 1990s, and especially since the advent of social media, Kusama has risen again. She is one of Japan's most important contemporary artists and one of the highest-selling female artists in the world.

Yusra Mardini

Swimmer
Born 5 March 1998
Syria

Olympic athletes compete as representatives of their nations; Yusra had dreamed of doing so since girlhood, and indeed, her dream came true – but not under her country's flag.

She grew up in Damascus, in a loving family. Her father, a swimming coach, taught Yusra and her sister Sara to swim. Yusra competed as a swimmer in Syria, but civil war broke out in 2011 and soon it became impossible to continue training: an unexploded bomb floating in the pool could force an evacuation.

In 2015, Sara and Yusra escaped to Lebanon, then to Turkey. There, along with eighteen other migrants, they boarded a dinghy – designed for seven people – bound for Greece. Shortly after setting off, the motor died, and water filled the boat. Sara, Yusra and two others jumped into the sea and began to swim, pushing the dinghy towards land. Yusra didn't know if she would survive but focused on a little boy aboard the boat; as she swam, she smiled at him so he wouldn't feel scared. Hours later, they reached the shore with no lives lost.

The sisters travelled to Berlin, where Yusra continued training with her coach, who lived there. News of her talent attracted the attention of the newly created Refugee Olympic Team, then recruiting for the Brazilian Games. Yusra competed in the Summer Olympics at Rio de Janeiro in the 100-metres freestyle and the 100-metres butterfly. Although she was worried about being viewed as an athlete selected out of pity rather than ability, the crowds changed her mind: she and her nation-less teammates were welcomed by thousands and treated with respect. Yusra was proud to be a refugee.

Mardini became the youngest-ever Goodwill Ambassador for the UN High Commissioner for Refugees, and she has written a book sharing her experiences. She hopes to compete at the Tokyo Olympics in 2021, representing millions of displaced people from around the world.

Zaha Hadid

Architect
31 October 1959 – 31 March 2016
Iraq and the United Kingdom

So singular was the vision of Zaha Hadid, one of the most exciting architects of the modern era, that for years she was considered a 'paper architect': a designer of fantastical buildings that would never be constructed. Hadid had a unique relationship with space and geometry; her buildings reconceived the possibilities for materials such as concrete and glass. She was called 'Queen of the Curve' for her fluid, undulating buildings, and was nicknamed 'the inventor of the 89 degrees' by her teachers at the Architectural Association in London. Her outlook was avant-garde, optimistic, innovative and visually striking, with a focus on abundant public space, civic utility and easy navigability. She was a boundary-breaker, and adamant about bringing buildings forth, uncompromised, from her imagination.

As an Arab woman working in what was then a boys' club, she learned to stay true to herself. Direct and hard-nosed with a flamboyant streak, she was defiant even amid criticism and controversy. Born in Baghdad to a family of industrialists and intellectuals, she studied mathematics in Beirut before moving to London to pursue a career in architecture. In 1979, she opened her own firm in London, which is still thriving today, with 400 employees. Her reputation grew and she won competitions. Soon after her first building, a fire station, was realised in 1989, her designs sprung up across the world. Over fifty of her building projects were completed in all – from the London Olympic Aquatics Centre and Rome's MAXXI museum to the Guangzhou Opera House.

Hadid was the recipient of a dizzying array of awards and honours and was the first woman and Muslim to win the Pritzker Prize, the profession's highest accolade. In 2016, she became the first woman to win the Royal Institute of British Architects' Royal Gold Medal, and she won the RIBA's Stirling Prize twice.

About the Author

Maliha Abidi is a Pakistani-American artist and illustrator whose work is primarily focused on women's rights, mental health and anti-racism. Born and raised in Karachi, Pakistan, Maliha emigrated to California, United States, at the age of fourteen, before eventually relocating to the UK.

Maliha's debut publication, *Pakistan for Women: Stories of Women Who Have Achieved Something Extraordinary* (2019), brought together the stories of fifty inspirational Pakistani women alongside their portrait illustrations. The first book of its kind to be published in Pakistan, it won Maliha international acclaim and appearances on the BBC, *Good Morning America* and TRT World, among others.

Maliha has since worked with several international organisations, including UNHCR, Women's Aid, the Malala Fund and the Peace Corporation, to showcase underrepresented narratives and help create positive change through art.

She is the founder of The Story of Mental Health (SOMH), an organisation providing resources on intersectional mental health awareness. SOMH is dedicated to creating a safe space for women to not only seek help, but also to work on their mental health creatively. The organisation is dedicated to working in countries and communities of colour, including in Pakistan, India, Bangladesh and Nepal, where stigma surrounds even the most basic discussions around mental health.

Maliha is currently pursuing a BSc in Neuroscience in California.

Acknowledgments

Writing this book has been quite a journey. I first began work on this project back in the summer of 2019, and it has taken about two years for it to become a reality.

There are so many in my life without whom this project might not have come to fruition. First and foremost, I am forever grateful to the two men in my life who constantly have my back. The first is my father, Jawaid Abidi, who has always encouraged me to follow my passions, and who continues to support me in all my endeavours. The second is my husband, Askari. There are times when I do not have the strength to believe in myself and, always, I have Aski beside me who reminds me why I should. They are my rocks.

I cannot thank my editor and publisher Lynn Gaspard enough. I think she should have been one of the women featured in *Rise*. I have learned a lot from her and am grateful that she believed in me, my writing and my art, and published this book. At Saqi, I would also like to thank Elizabeth Briggs, whose keen eye for detail and passion for the book were invaluable to me. I loved working with her and am ever so thankful for her support.

From the beginning, Lynn and I decided that the book should include stories of women from around the world, and that these should be of both famous women and those who may not yet be household names, but whose impact is unforgettable. A lot of research went into this, and here, I must thank Jessica Horn of 'Still She Rises', who provided invaluable guidance and insight on the women in this book from sub-Saharan Africa.

Finally, I have found so much strength in the stories of the 100 remarkable women in this book, who paved the way for millions of us. I am excited that they can now be a source of inspiration, empowerment and strength for readers worldwide.

Saqi Books
26 Westbourne Grove, London W2 5RH
www.saqibooks.com

First published 2021 by Saqi Books

A full CIP record for this book is available from the British Library.

ISBN 9780863561375
EISBN 9780863561672

Printed by PBtisk a.s.

LOTTERY FUNDED

Supported using public funding by

**ARTS COUNCIL
ENGLAND**